ENDORSEMENTS

"Despite the provocative title, *The Secrets - How To Control A Man*, is a user friendly, well written guide to truly captivating and capturing a man's heart, mind, and body. Mr. Cost condenses a wealth of experience and practical knowledge into a concise easy to read book. Feminist may find it too traditional, but post feminist may find it refreshing. Women fed up with men will undoubtedly read *The Secrets* with keen interest and appreciation."

Dr. Seth Farber, Ph.D. Psychology, Author of: Madness, Heresy and The Rumors of Angels, Guest on: The Oprah Winfrey Show, Geraldo, and William F. Buckley's Firing Line

"If I were dating a woman who followed the advice given in *The Secrets*, I would do everything in my power to give her anything she wanted!"

Rudy Simms, Author of: Double Speak In Black & White

"Hilarious! You'll either love it or hate it. Either way it will make you 'think'"

Reverend Dr. Philip Valentine, HHC: ND, Author of:
The Wounded Womb

"Mr. Cost has written a noteworthy and informative book - especially useful if one works with women as I do. I recommend it to all of my colleagues as well as women seeking to connect in a meaningful relationship. Peace and Love!

John V. Staton, NCPSYA, Psychotherapist - NYC

"*The Secrets* are out! I love your book! It's like a back-stage view of male sexual secrets. Thank you for a book written with personal - private language, not scientific - pornographic language. It's written so women on all levels can read, smile, and experiment with their sexual experiences. However, the title does not do justice to the material of the book. Your book shared your lovemaking experiences very tenderly, non violently and non-mechanically. Simply p̶ ̶ ̶ ̶ ̶ ̶ ̶ ̶ ̶ ̶ ̶ ̶ ̶ ̶ other happy. Just reading *The Secrets* ma

Harriett Walthall, Educator, N

"*The Secrets* is a wonderful book! It teaches women in a clear step by step approach how to really please a man and ultimately control him. Many books have been written on relationships, but none of them are as honest and detailed as C.E. Cost's The Secrets. This book builds a woman's confidence in her ability to effectively deal with men. As a Brazilian woman I feel that the ideas Mr. Cost presents also applies to Brazilian men and men in general. Every woman needs to read *The Secrets*."

Leticia Breda, Manager

"This book is incredibly accurate with regards to the issues it addresses. We can't wait for it to be published so that we can get our copy of the actual book!"

Kimberly Mullis & Michael Gray, Horse Groomer, Iron Worker

"I love your book! The advice you give will help make better relationships between women and men. It will also save lots of marriages"

Indra Gajramsing, Child Care Provider

"C.E. Cost delves into what men really want. He tells the truth about how to hook the man of your dreams. You must read this "no-nonsense" approach to pleasing a man! In return, a woman will get a man who would be a fool to stray. Men have used prostitutes since the beginning of time so that they could get exactly what they want. Reading this book will show you how you can be the only lover he'll ever want. Even though this book is directed towards women, as a gay man I must confess that I agree with the techniques shared in this book and I learned some new tips to keep my life-partner happy. You need to share this book with your best friend!"

Rich Kennedy, Producer of the radio talk show, "Passion Phones - Real Radio" Orlando, Florida

The Secrets

HOW TO CONTROL A MAN

C. E. COST

THE SECRETS PUBLISHING INC.

Visit us at: thesecretsrevealed.com

The Secrets Publishing Inc.
2230 Cascades Blvd. Suite 106
Kissimmee, FL 34741
(407) 847-3583

Also: www.thesecretsrevealed.com

Become a member and share your views with others

Cover design by Mshindo I, (718)452-7936 and
Reverend Dr. Philip Valentine, (718)264-9497
Chapter illustrations by Mshindo I
Text design by John Cole Graphic Designer, (505)466-4290

PLEASE NOTE

While the author is confident that readers will find the information presented here to be very helpful, it is the responsibility of
each individual to decide what they feel comfortable trying.

The author is available for interviews and lectures.

CONTENTS

INTRODUCTION

WHAT QUALIFIES ME TO WRITE ON THIS TOPIC

To begin with, I am a man and only a man really knows what things a woman can do to really please a man. In addition, just like women, men do get together and share their experiences. Men constantly complain about the same types of things that women do or don't do. Furthermore, I have been blessed to have dated a wide variety of beautiful, sensuous women, from a variety of cultures, educational and professional backgrounds. I have dated women that most men only dream about. I know the difference between okay sex and explosive dynamic sex. I know what a woman can do when she really wants to please a man. I have also spent a lot of time over the years reading books and articles on sex and relationships. Some of what I read I thought was good, but most of it I felt was impractical and from a woman's perspective. Even the books written by men seemed geared more to telling women the types of things they wanted to hear rather than getting down to hard-core issues. I therefore felt that there was a need for something simple, practical and did not pull any punches. Here I get down and dirty with nothing held back and from a man's perspective. If you doubt how effective The Secrets are, then give a copy of this book to a man you trust and ask him how he would feel about a woman who followed the recommendations in this book. Even better, put the guidelines written here into practice and see what happens.

Lots of women, if not the majority, are suffering out there because they keep making the same mistakes over and over again. They think they know what men want based on things they have heard from their female friends, or read in some romance novel, or seen in the movies, but they still end up bitterly disappointed. They ultimately conclude that all men are no good, because they have tried everything they thought they were supposed to do. The problem is not that men are all bad, but that men don't tell women what they are doing wrong. Even if a woman were to ask a man to make a list of what she needed to do to please him more, the average man would not list everything. He would be too afraid of getting into an argument. Furthermore, he may be too embarrassed to tell her certain things. In addition, he may not be able to articulate everything, but he just has an awkward feeling about some of the things she does or does not do. Therefore, what I reveal in The Secrets, for the most part, every man already knows, even though he doesn't tell his wife or girlfriend. The Secrets are only secrets to most women.

I have had many men and women read The Secrets before its publication, and the responses were overwhelming. At first I was concerned that men would complain about me revealing too much, but I got the exact opposite response. They were grateful that someone was finally telling women what they needed to know. One guy I feel summarized the reactions of the others. I asked him, if a woman followed the guidelines in The Secrets, would he appreciate her more? His response was an enthusiastic: "Hell, yeah!" The responses from the women were equally strong. One woman commented: "I've been doing everything all wrong!" Another noted: "Now I know my mistakes." Another woman was so stunned by how much I revealed she asked: "Whose side are you on?" These reactions were from college educated, professional women, who subscribe to all types of women's magazines and read all kinds of books on sex and relationships.

These comments, as well as that of many others helped me to satisfy myself that I was on target and that the guidelines I provide are helpful. This was my ultimate goal in revealing The Secrets. Each day too many women wake up frustrated and angry about the relationship they are in. Either they are constantly arguing with their mate or they can't get him to respond in ways they want. Life is too short to live it in constant misery. A lot of time that could be spent fucking, sharing magical moments, and starting happy families is wasted needlessly. Regardless of what has happened in the past, The Secrets can open the door to new possibilities for you.

WHAT IS CONTROL?

You want certain things from a man such as sex, money, companionship, marriage, a family etc. For the purposes of this book, by control I simply mean *a woman's ability to get the things she wants from a man.* What you want from a man is up to you and your conscience, but knowing what you want from a man and how to get it is what control is all about. If you know *The Secrets,* a man will be a happy participant eager to grant your requests and desires.

It is easy for the average woman to get the average man into bed, but how long can she keep him there? It is also easy for many women to manipulate men they don't care about, but how good are they when it comes to men they really want and care about? My goal in creating The Secrets is to show women how to go beyond short-term and simple manipulations to going after and keeping the men they really want and getting what they really want from these men. This is real control!

2

TREAT HIM INCONSISTENTLY

If you are consistently nice to your lover or consistently bad to your lover, it is easier for him to leave you. But if you treat him inconsistently, he will stay attached to you far longer. Psychologists have known this for many years. You have done this unconsciously with individuals that you didn't care about that much and it is these same people who ended up, to your amazement, falling in love with you. You thought about how badly you treated that person, and you asked yourself: "How could he be in love with me after the way I have treated him."

The reason why he "loves" you is the same reason why a woman who is routinely beaten by her husband or boyfriend stays with that person. It is because he treats her inconsistently. After he beats her, he later makes up and treats her very kindly and affectionately. He might treat her very lovingly for the next few weeks or even the next few months, but he will eventually go back to beating her. It is this on again/off again, up/down, hot/cold cycle that compels her to stay with him! She really believes that she is in love with him and that she can control him, and change him so that he is nice to her all of the time. She also sincerely believes that he really loves her. Little does she realize that she is merely the victim of psychological manipulation!

HOW TO BE INCONSISTENT
WHEN YOU ARE NICE, BE REALLY NICE

- **Take him out to clubs.** Dance and party. Get him a little drunk and then go home with him and fuck his brains out! Make it a night to remember.

- **Invite him out to dinner.** Find out what kind of food he likes and take him to those types of restaurants. Try to find special out of the way places where the setting is romantic and the food is delicious. It is not necessary to always go to expensive, fancy places. Most guys are simple creatures who are easy to please.

- **Cook for him on occasion.** A woman who can cook dishes that her lover really likes is worth many times her weight in gold. How quickly is a guy going to give up a woman who knows how to make delicious meals that he can't find anywhere else? Buy several different types of cookbooks and learn how to cook Italian, French, Brazilian, Thai, African American, Mexican and other types of dishes. Experiment with your own special touches to create truly unique dishes that only you can make.

- **Buy him little gifts now and then.** They don't have to be expensive, just simple little things that you know he likes. A girl I dated knew that I liked Brazilian music and so now and then she would buy me a Brazilian CD which I appreciated immensely since she knew which Brazilian artists were best. Other things could include a poem, a tie etc. Keep it simple, unique and personal as much as possible. Don't do this every week, but now and then.

HOW TO BE BAD

The simplest way to do this is to change the way you think about the guy you want. You may think that you are deeply in love with him, you can't live without him, he is the only man in the world for you as ordained by God, but the reality is he is just an ordinary guy. You will most likely "fall in love" with several other guys before you go to your grave. Forget about finding that one person you believe that you were destined to be with. Forget about soul mates and all of those other nice, cute ideas you find in romance novels. Take it from me, I have been in love with women I thought I could not be without. Yet, I would later meet someone else even more beautiful, charming and sweeter than my previous "love".

You must remember that there are literally millions of men in the world who could make you happy and fulfill all of your desires and needs. You pass them everyday on the street, but they are too afraid to approach you or you are often too afraid to talk them or give your number to the ones who do take a chance and approach you. On many occasions, you may have underestimated the guy who is trying to talk to you or there might be some simple thing about him, which may have turned you off from him, even though he could have been perfect for you if you gave him a chance.

If you are too infatuated with a man, the key is to take him off of that pedestal that you have put him on and bring him down to earth with us mortal men. It may help if you imagined him sitting on the toilet, or picking his nose, or passing gas or doing something else that is crude or awkward that makes you laugh and reminds you that he is just a guy. If you change the way you see him, you won't be calling him every five minutes or worrying about why he hasn't called you yet. Relax. Take it easy. He is only a guy! You can also try imaging that he is some guy you don't care that much about, but who has a crush on you. How would you normally treat such a person? That is exactly how you should treat your lover or the guy you want to be your lover if you know that you are too obsessed with him. It takes will power, but it is worth it in the end.

- **Be late for dates on occasion.** Just make sure that you have a good, believable excuse as to why you are late, such as you got caught in traffic, the train was late, you could not find your keys or anything that is reasonable. Make sure that you are always nice and apologetic when you are late.

- **Cancel dates at the last minute on occasion.** You must be a little unpredictable. Make sure that you have a good excuse and be nice!

- **You end the telephone conversations before he does.** This keeps you in control and keeps him wanting more time with you.

- **Don't return all of his calls immediately.** Sometimes make him wait a few hours or a day or two. Let me stress that you don't do this all of the time, but only once in a while.

- **Deny him sex on occasion.** Make sure that you have a good excuse and you are nice about it. Don't act like you don't care about his sexual desires, or that you are deliberately trying to manipulate him. Maybe you had a long hard day at work. Maybe you are not feeling well. Maybe you are depressed about something. Be a good actress! Make it believable. You should not do this to him on a regular basis, but only now and then. You don't want him to feel that he can't count on you when he wants sex, but rather he should feel a slight uncertainty. Make it up to him the next time by giving him the best sex he has had in a long time. If you already know his hot buttons then push them. In addition, try something kinky to add some extra spice. If you treat him like this, he won't mind so much when you deny him sex once in a while. You will eventually have him wrapped around your finger.

ELIMINATE ALL PRESSURE

Don't ask him how he feels about you. Let him tell you how he feels about you. The quickest way to drive a man away is by putting pressure on him. By doing this you are pushing him into a corner and his only choice is to seek an escape route. Even if he tells you that he cares about you or that he loves you, under this condition you can't trust what he tells you. If he likes your body and enjoys fucking you and he likes your company, do you really think that the average guy is going to risk losing you by saying the wrong thing? It is much easier for him to give you a few reassuring words to get you off of his back and then change the subject.

Don't tell him how you feel about him. This is another form of pressure. What you are really doing is saying: "I can't stand not knowing how you feel about me anymore, so I'm going to tell you how strong I feel about you and you to tell me that you feel the same about me." This is an act of desperation. You are putting him on the spot, which he will interpret as unwanted pressure. Again it would be better to let him initiate this. Wait until he tells you how he feels.

The reality is you both have a very good idea about how you each feel about each other by the amount of time that you spend together and the quality of the time you are together. If you are having fun conversations on the phone everyday when you are not together, if you are seeing each other several times a week and you are having a great time each time you are together, and you both are having explosive orgasms in various sexual positions, do you really need to ask him how does he feel?

If you are feeling a burning desire to tell him how you feel or ask him how he feels, that is a sure sign that something is wrong. You probably are sensing that he is not as much into you as you are into him. Maybe he is not calling you enough, or he's not taking you out enough, or he's doing something else that causes you to feel insecure. He may have feelings for another woman, you may have bad breath, you may not be fulfilling him sexually, maybe you talk too much, maybe you are too possessive and jealous. There could be a lot of reasons why he is not giving you his all, but the worst thing you can do is to pressure him into expressing warm, fuzzy feelings about you. It is okay to show your feelings, but don't tell him how you feel or ask him how he feels. Don't even talk or ask him about how your relationship is going unless he starts the conversation about this. Let him initiate this. When it happens it will probably be one joyful moment when he spontaneously tells you that he loves you!

Therefore, instead of applying pressure, make him dependent on you because you are the one who is not putting any pressure on him. You make him feel good without nagging him. He likes talking to you, because you care about his opinions and you really listen. Even if he is seeing another woman, he is going to enjoy being with you more and more.

HOW TO KISS HIM

Remove all lipstick and facial makeup before kissing. Digesting all of those chemicals while you and your man are kissing is not good for the health of either of you. If you doubt how harmful cosmetics are, get a book entitled: A Consumer's Dictionary of Cosmetic Ingredients by Ruth Winter. In the introduction of her book, she notes:

> There is no toxicity information available for 56% of the cosmetic ingredients and 28% have less than minimal information and only 2 percent have complete health hazard assessment.... A number of cosmetic ingredients now in use have been shown to be carcinogenic in animals or to cause genetic breaks in cells.

You can also go on the Internet and search for websites on this subject by typing in "cosmetic ingredients dangers". Better yet, avoid wearing lipstick and a lot of makeup if you anticipate the possibility that you are going to be kissing later in the evening. Make sure that your breath absolutely smells good or neutral. Strong breath fresheners aren't too appealing either. Have a few drinks so that you both can relax and you can get nice and juicy. Let him take the lead in kissing for the most part. Do not ram your tongue in his mouth. Go slow. Suck on his lips. Allow your tongue to twirl lightly around his tongue. Act shy like it is your first time as you allow his tongue to probe deeper into your mouth or as you slowly probe deeper into his mouth. Kiss him on the cheeks, nose, eyelids, and forehead.

Flick his ear lobes with your tongue, and then begin to slowly suck his ear lobes. This will drive him crazy! Kiss and run your tongue along the side of his neck to the part that meets his shoulder. This is where vampires in the movies bite the women and they submit in a state of ecstasy! It is no accident that that spot was chosen. It is one of the hot spots on the body for women and men. Lick and suck slowly on that part of his neck and see for yourself how wild this drives him. As you continue to kiss him, your hands should gently fondle his arms, shoulders, chest, neck and of course his dick. Run your fingers through his hair, gently scratching and massaging his head. Moan and make other sensual sounds. Tell him what a great kisser he is. Move your body in rhythmic, sexy, turned on motions while rubbing your breasts and thighs up against him. If you kiss like this be prepared to be fucked long and hard. He will enjoy kissing you almost as much as he enjoys making love to you.

SEX - HOW TO FUCK HIM!

Scream a lot! Why do you think that men prefer younger women? It is largely because they scream and moan more! It is exciting for a man to hear a woman screaming and moaning as he pounds his dick inside her. It's a turn on. It makes a man's dick get harder and want to fuck longer and more intensely. Therefore, scream, moan and act like his cock is the biggest experience you have ever had.

TALK DIRTY DURING SEX

Talking dirty is another big turn on during sex. Say things like:
"Fuck me!"
"Fuck that pussy hard!"
"Yes Poppie! That's it Poppie!"
"Make me cum!"
"I like it hard"
"I love big dicks!"
"I love your big dick inside me!"
"Fuck me David! That's it, fuck me hard David"
"Abuse my pussy!"

DON'T MENTION LOVE DURING SEX

Don't talk about how much you love him while you are having sex. That is a different energy. Save the love talk for when you are holding hands at a candlelight dinner. If you start talking about love you are going to have him thinking about church, family and all sorts of things that water down a stiff hard-on. Talk dirty during sex and he will enjoy you more.

YOUR VOICE DURING SEX

Your voice should always be soft and seductive. This will keep him pounding away in ecstasy. Even when you are screaming from his banging the hell out of you, your voice should be more like a eighteen year old girl than a woman wrestler.

DON'T COMPLAIN

Never complain during sex. If you complain during sex he will lose his erection and then what will you do? If you are bored or tired of making love, don't let him know. Don't say things like "Are you finished?" "Are you almost there?" Never make him feel that you are rushing him. If you are really tired or bored or for whatever the reason, you want him to finish up quickly, just keep telling him to fuck you harder. Tell him how much you love it. Plead with him to go deeper inside you. Say things like: "More! More! More! Bang that pussy hard! Give it to me!" Moan, whimper, scream! Act like he is driving you crazy. The more turned on you act, the more excited he will get and the faster he will cum. In the process you might actually become more excited yourself.

SEXUAL POSITIONS

Try different sexual positions. If he is always on top, you ask if you could get on top. Do it doggy style if you haven't already. Try it sideways. Get a book on different sexual positions and experiment. You may have to get into a little better shape to do some of these positions. The following are a few suggestions.

DOGGIE STYLE

Doggy style is one of the most common positions and it is a lot of fun and easy to do. You are down on all fours with your legs opened for him to take you from behind. Let him choose the position and set the pace. When you are doing it doggy style, let him adjust how he wants to position you. If your butt is too high or too low, this could be awkward for him as he is fucking you. This largely depends on the height of both of you. Likewise, if you are leaning too far forward while you are in the doggy position, or too far backwards, this could be very uncomfortable for him as he is stroking in and out of you. Many women allow their man to adjust them instinctively, but others insist on deciding how they will situate themselves, and then they wonder why they are not being sexually gratified. Therefore let him adjust you in a way that is most comfortable for him. This will maximize his performance and your pleasure.

You should try to just remain still as he is thrusting inside you, so that you do not disrupt his rhythm. You don't want to work against him because you will wear him out quicker and he might lose his erection. Sometimes women become too excited and eager to have an organism and they start jerking and thrusting in wild ways that help themselves to cum, but in so doing they are messing up their man's ability to maintain his erection. Remember this, when it comes to sex, ultimately the man is the initiator and the woman is the recipient. The bottom line is, if the man loses his erection, no fucking is going to take place.

Some women know how to thrust in ways that actually enhances a man's sexual pleasure. They know how to move with his rhythm and not against it. While you are in the doggy position, when he is pulling out, you should pull forward slightly, and when he is pushing back inside you, you should push backwards slightly. You don't want to pull too far forward or push too far backwards because again you don't want to throw him off. Likewise you don't want to thrust too hard for the same reason. You have to experiment with this to get a feel for what is just right. Your goal should always be to work in harmony with your man when you are doing it doggy style or any other position.

When you are in the doggy position or any other position, always talk dirty, moan and scream! Tell him how much you like his big dick. Tell him how much you love his huge cock deep inside you. Always make him feel like he is a jock. The more you make him feel like a stud the more he will become one. Keep telling him to fuck you hard! Sex is not the time to hold back or try to act dignified. Save the dignity for cocktail parties. Sex is the time for you to get down and dirty. Even if you have never talked like this to your man before, he won't know what got into you, but he will love it! The dirtier you talk the harder he'll fuck! I am emphasizing this because it is extremely important if you want to maximize his pleasure and ultimately yours. Great sex is a critical key in controlling a man.

MISSIONARY POSITION

This is the most common sexual position in which the man is on top and the woman is on bottom. You should keep your legs wide apart and up in the air such that the bottoms of your feet are pointed towards the ceiling. Ideally, the closer you can bring your knees towards your shoulders the better. This will make it much easier for him to penetrate you deeply. In addition, when you are in this position, you seem more vulnerable yet receptive. This is a tremendous turn on for guys.

The first woman I ever made love to raised her knees all the way up to her shoulders and used her hands to hold her legs in place. I was able to freely pound away inside her. To this day I remember her very vividly. A lot of women are not in good enough shape to raise their legs that high. If that is the case for you, then you need to exercise more and stretch more. You will increase his pleasure and yours when he makes love to you in this position.

Do not lock your legs around his when you are in the missionary position. Some women get too excited and lock their legs around their man's. When this happens, every time he lifts up he is fighting against the strength of your legs pulling down on his. This taps his strength and throws off his rhythm. If you want, you can rest your legs lightly on the back of his, so long as you don't apply any pressure to the back of his legs.

You should either remain still as he fucks you or move to his rhythm. You don't want to do anything that would inhibit his rhythm because if you inhibit his rhythm, he will lose his erection, or he will not have the explosive orgasm he was shooting for. Do not jerk to the left or the right or up or down. Remember that he is going in and out. If you move in any other direction, you are throwing him off. Avoid jerky motions; instead become in tuned with his rhythm and pace yourself with him - not against him.

One variation on the missionary position is when he is on top, but his arms are on the bed supporting his weight and elevating his chest a foot or so above you. While you are lying there on your back you should gently caress and stroke his chest, stomach and ribs with your fingertips. You can also use your nails to lightly scratch the surface of his skin. Lick and kiss his neck and shoulders. Suck on his ear lobes. While you are doing this you should be moaning, whimpering and talking dirty.

Another variation on the missionary position is for you to be on top facing down on him. A common mistake women make in this position is again that they get too excited too quickly and start pumping too hard which throws off his rhythm. You would do better to go slow and rhythmically. Go all the way down on his dick slowly and all the way up slowly. As he becomes more excited he will start thrusting inside you. You should then adjust to his rhythm. One woman I was with did this better than any other I have ever been with. I'll call her Betsy. She would slowly descend down on me, but she would only go halfway and then slowly pull up. By not going all the way down she was teasing the hell out of me. Betsy would stare down at me, looking me directly in the eyes. Her eyelids were half opened and she had this sexually intoxicated look in her eyes. Her large breasts were dangling in front of me. She would reach down periodically and give me a light juicy kiss. She never changed her pace. She took her time and kept going only halfway down on me and back up. Betsy knew exactly what she was doing to me. I was trying to exercise willpower, because it felt so good, I wanted it to last. I held out as long as I could and then I began banging away as hard and as deeply as I could. She knew how to give me her own unique brand of pleasure. I remember her very vividly to this day.

You should feel free to experiment with ways of stroking your man to enhance his pleasure and yours when you are on top. Make sure that you rub your tits up and down on face and chest. Tell him: "My nipples are so hot, they need to be sucked", and then take your breast in your hand and put your nipple in his mouth. Moan as he sucks on it. Tell him how good it feels. Your eyes should have that half opened, intoxicated, look, as if you have lost yourself in raw sexual passion and you are his sexual toy and there is nothing you can do about it. When you do this be prepared for the sexual fire you have ignited.

STANDING POSITION

Lean on a dresser or the bed with your butt sticking out and allow him to take you from behind. Experiment with how far your legs are apart. Sometimes have them far apart so that you are wide open for him and at other times keep your legs close together. Each position creates different stimulating sensations for him and you. This also applies when you are doing it doggy style. Unless he adjusts you to a specific position, vary how wide you open your legs when he is making love to you in this way. The standing position is a nice change from always doing it in bed. As always, make sure you moan, talk dirty and move to his rhythm.

For more ideas about sexual positions you should get Anne Hooper's book: Kama Sutra - Classic Love Making Techniques For Today's Lover's. You should also get Nitya Lacroix's book: Love, Sex & Intimacy. These books feature graphic color illustrations of various positions. Your local bookstore should have many other books on sexual positions.

ORAL SEX

Men love this when it is done right. Go slow at first and at the same time stroking his penis with your hand. Moan as you do this. Say things like "Your cock is so big". "I love your big dick in my mouth". "I want you to cum all over my face".

If he has foreskin because he was not circumcised, you must be careful not to pull it too far back because this could be irritating or even painful to him. Either suck over the foreskin or only pull the foreskin partly back.

Slowly slide your tongue up and down and all around his dick like it is a delicious piece of candy. Take his dick deeply into your mouth sucking on it slowly in and out...in and out. Stroke his balls and thighs lightly with your fingertips. Take your time. Don't try to rush this. You want him to enjoy every moment of having his big dick going slowly and deeply into your warm, wet innocent mouth, and partly out again. Listen to the sounds that he is making. Is he moaning? Is he talking dirty saying things like "Oh shit", "You're the best" "You're driving me out of my fucking mind!" Is he starting to have muscle spasms as he starts to thrust his dick inside your mouth? These are indicators that he is really enjoying himself and is on the verge of cumming. Wait until you are sure he is starting to cum and then stroke his cock a little faster with your hand. Always be gentle as you do this. At the same time start to suck his dick harder and harder taking his whole cock into your mouth deeper and faster.

When he cums, don't pull away! If you do, you will mess up his orgasm. It may seem disgusting and dirty if it is your first time, but at one time you probably also thought that any form of sex was dirty too. Imagine how you would feel if a guy is masterfully stroking your clitoris with his tongue and you were on the verge of an explosive organism, but then suddenly he pulls away in disgust! That is how a guy feels when a woman pulls away while he is coming during oral sex. Let him complete what you started. Continue to suck hungrily on his hard dick until you drain him dry. This will drive him wild and he will view you as a sexual Goddess -a rare and precious woman he must keep. Think of how you would feel about a guy who knew how to consistently give you great organisms just with his tongue!

From my experience, very few women know how to give really good blowjobs, just like most guys don't know how to bring a woman to a single orgasm, much less have multiple orgasms. (Don't worry, my next book will teach the guys what to do to drive you into a sexual frenzy). The few women I have been with who knew how to give great head were as precious as gold to me. For additional tips, rent or buy a bunch of adult videos and study how the professional women do it. This little investment will yield huge dividends for you.

ANAL SEX

Many guys like to do this on occasion with their woman just to do something different. Let him. Use plenty of lubrication of course, such as KY Gel and just relax and take it slow. Let him know if you are feeling some unbearable pain at first and ask him to go slower or if necessary ask him to pull out for a few moments until you feel comfortable and then have him put his dick back in. By allowing him to have this experience with you, you reduce his need to find another woman who will allow him to have this experience. After you get over the initial reluctance and discomfort from trying something new, you will probably find it to be very stimulating and a lot of fun. A survey in Cosmopolitan (August 2001, p. 166) found that 41% of the women surveyed said that they had anal sex. Contrary to what you might think, a woman can achieve an explosive orgasm through anal sex.

ADULT VIDEOS

In addition to teaching you about oral sex, adult videos can teach you a lot about positions and other things you can do to improve your sexual performance. Don't be embarrassed about renting or buying adult videos. View them as graphic instructional guides, which will enable you to make the guy you want even happier in bed. Take note of what the women do to drive the guys wild. Try out some of the things you learn.

BE A GOOD ACTRESS IN SEX

If you don't have an orgasm, fake it. Lie. Tell him how good he was. Just make him feel like he rocked your world. If you do, he will be more willing to try things you suggest that really will bring you to have explosive orgasms. Act like an eighteen-year-old girl. This drives men wild. Moan when he touches your breast or licks your nipples. Part of the thrill for a man in feeling and sucking on a woman's breasts and nipples, is her response when he does this. One girl I was with, from the moment I started licking her nipples her knees buckled, her head, arms, and back flung backwards towards the floor like she was going to faint and she started moaning. The only thing that prevented her from falling to the floor was me catching her. She was in her own world of ecstasy. My dick got immediately hard and I couldn't wait to fuck her!

Even if it is not your first time, pretend like it is. Act like a teenage girl with little to no experience with sex. Your whole body should be sensitive to the touch. Moan, tremble, scream, dig your nails into his back (not too deeply)! I once dated a woman who I will call "Joleen". She told me that she had a lot of other boyfriends. In addition, she had a slightly tough exterior, but once she was naked, she melted like butter in my arms. She moaned and trembled when I sucked her breasts, or ran my hand up and down her thighs. Her whole body was sensitive to the touch like she was a virgin. Therefore, always act like a virgin.

When you act like you are just going through the motions when you are having sex with your lover, he will get bored and start to seek another more thrilling sexual partner on the side, even if he has to pay for it. Sex with you just becomes more of his duty than a burning desire he has for you. This happens all the time in marriages. If women just screamed more and acted like shy 18-year-old virgins or at least recent virgins, their men would have less of a need to seek sex from other women.

TOUCH

Touch him often. Stroke his hands, arm and neck. Massage his hands with lotion. Do his nails. Run your fingers along the back of his ears. This will endear him to you.

MASSAGE & SEX

Constantly give him massages. If you massage him before sex, he will be more relaxed and perform better. On other occasions massage him after sex. This will endear him to you because few women will do this and most don't know how. Most women spend hundreds of dollars on perfume, makeup, hairstyles, dresses and jewelry to impress their man, or the man they want to get, but they will refuse to give him a massage. By giving massages, this will make you very special and valuable to him. Think about it, what feels better than a nice full body massage with warm massage oil after having delicious sex? If you don't know how to give good massages then buy a book on the subject or take a class. It will be well worth it. An easy way to give good massages is to think about what you would like done if someone was giving you a massage and then do it to him. Don't be afraid to apply extra pressure. A man's body is obviously stronger than a woman's body and he needs a little more pressure to really enjoy it. If you give a massage too softly, you are not maximizing his pleasure. Massage him often.

KINKY IS GOOD

As already mentioned, there is nothing worst for a relationship than boring, same old routine sex. Therefore, surprise your man with different little things designed to tease and excite him. Be creative. For example, I dated one woman who always had stimulating surprises for me. I decided one day to call her at her job and invite her over after work for a candlelight dinner. When she arrived she took a shower and came out of the shower with only a towel wrapped around her waist. Her large, beautiful sensitive breasts always drove me crazy and she knew it. She calmly sat at the table eating with those two huge mounds staring me in the face. I tried, but she wouldn't let me fuck her. I was going crazy, but there was nothing I could do. I had to sit there for the entire meal with her tits dangling in my face as she carried on a casual conversation with me as if nothing out of the ordinary was happening. When we finally finished eating and I got her in bed, I was like a wild animal just let out of a cage. I fucked her harder than I think I had any other woman, as she moaned: "Oh…fuck that pussy!"

Another woman I was with, got down on all fours and told me to spank her so that she could get good and wet. She moaned sweetly. She then climbed on top of me with her big beautiful ass in my face as she proceeded to teach me how great oral sex can really be.

HOW TO BE KINKY

When your man shows up at your door, greet him completely naked except for a pair of high heel shoes and a black choker around your neck.

While watching television or listening to music or whatever you and your man are doing, suddenly and without a word, get undressed and get down on all fours on the sofa or the floor, with your legs wide apart and your butt in the air facing him. Don't say a word. Let him figure out how to handle the situation!

Greet him one day with an attractive girlfriend of yours or a professional, and you both fuck him. A survey in Cosmopolitan (August 2001, p.166) found that 12% of the women had sex with a man and another woman. If this is a true measure of society at large, that would mean that for every 1 million American women, roughly 120,000 of them have had "two girls/one guy sex". If you have enough confidence in yourself and your relationship to do this, then you will be giving him the thrill of a lifetime. Men fantasize about what it would be like to have two women at the same time. Every man has dreamt about what it would be like to be James Bond or Hugh Heffner. You would be fulfilling that dream for him. It would be the ultimate Christmas and birthday gift wrapped into one. In addition, you will probably learn some things about what he likes and how to please him.

HAVE SEX IN PUBLIC PLACES

I once made love to a girlfriend of mine in Central Park at 2 o'clock in the morning. I loved every minute of it and it was an experience that will be etched into my memory forever. There is something about the risk of getting caught that makes it especially exciting. Another girlfriend and I one night we went to the roof to look at the stars and as we started back down the stairs a hot flash came over us and we made love on the staircase. I know it sounds crazy, but we got away with it and it was a hell of a lot of fun.

Try to pick a spot and a time of day that would give you both a reasonable amount of time to finish screwing before someone actually spotted you. If you are caught just keep fucking anyway! You will remember it for the rest of your life because of the embarrassment and excitement of the whole experience. Fuck him in the shower or while taking a bath. Do a strip tease for him by candlelight with soft music playing. Remove your clothes slowly as you squeeze your breasts in front of him. Rub your hands up and down your thighs and across your belly as you jiggle and shake and twirl your delicious body before his hungry eyes.

If you bring kinkyness into your sexual relationship you will turn your relationship into a sexual adventure for him. He will be too busy thinking about what you will come up with next to think about another woman or anything else that would distract him from appreciating and enjoying you. Every woman comes with the same basic equipment, but it is how you use it or flaunt it that really counts. It is what makes you unique, special, and precious to a man. Be Kinky!

TALK DIRTY IN DIFFERENT SETTINGS

While at a club, or eating dinner at a restaurant, or watching a movie, take his hand and look him straight in the eyes and tell him:

"I want you to fuck the shit out of me!"

"I want to suck your big dick!"

"I want you to ram your big cock in my mouth!"

"I need you to fuck my ass!"

"I deserve to be spanked real hard because I have been a bad girl. Then I want you to fuck me real good."

These are some of the things that the women who turned me on the most have said to me. Talking dirty drives men crazy. He'll be dying to get you home and into bed. Make these types of requests with conviction and passion! You are hot! You are sexy! You need him badly!

7

SEX WITH YOU— HOW TO MEASURE HIS EXCITEMENT

If he is quietly fucking you with steady controlled strokes, he is thinking about another woman or women. Sex with you is somewhere between boring and okay. For the most part he is just fulfilling his obligations as a boyfriend or husband. A man who really enjoys sex with you is fucking you in an out of controlled, lustful way. He doesn't just fuck you hard, he is having virtually uncontrolled muscle spasms. Something has taken over him. You have unleashed the animal in him! Even if he is screwing you slowly, he is grinding deeper and deeper inside you. Every inch of his hungry cock wants to enjoy your sweet, tight, wet, innocent pussy. He is moaning and saying things like: "Baby you give it up so good!" "You're driving me crazy", "You make my dick so hard". When he cums it is not like a mild tremor, but rather it is a massive volcanic explosion! He is yelling his head off as he unleashes all of the sexual fury that you have ignited in him. If a man has a nice quiet orgasm while making love to you, he is bored. You did not arouse him to the highest heights. Trust me on this. I have dated far more women from diverse backgrounds and cultures than most men have. I know how it feels and how I respond when a woman really drives me crazy. My girlfriend Diana (don't worry, this is not her real name) knew exactly what buttons to push to always drive me crazy. For example, she always talked dirty to me. She kept egging me on by saying things like: "Fuck me harder!" "Give it to me!" No matter how hard I thrust she demanded more. This would drive me out of my mind! She also found out that I had a thing for Latin woman, so she would say things like: "Yes Poppie! Give it to me hard Poppie!" She did this even though she was not Spanish! The average woman would never do this, but Diana was well above average and she always sent me into an intense sexual frenzy! At times I did not know where I got the energy from. She always had me yelling when I was cumming. It was embarrassing, because all of the neighbors knew when we were going at it. I could not help myself. Diana knew how to inflame my passions.

If you want to see the difference for yourself, get a stack of adult videos and pay attention to the men in those videos. You will be able to spot the ones who are just going through the motions and are just doing it for the money, versus the ones who are really into it!

Another marker to look for is how often he wants to fuck you. If he wants to screw you two or three times in a night, that is a good sign. If he does it once and then he is ready to turnover and go to sleep for the night or go watch television, this is a warning sign. If he has no problem with skipping a few days or worse a few weeks without pestering you about doing the wild thing, this is a warning sign. Of course this varies depending on the man's age, health, and the longevity of his relationship with you. In general though, the more a man wants to make love to you, the more you can rest assured that he is really enjoying you sexually.

Once you have an idea of how much a man is enjoying his sexual experience with you, you have an idea of how hard you have to work. Reread the chapter on *How To Fuck Him*. If stamina and being overweight is part of his problem or your problem, then work out a schedule for both of you to go to the gym together. Get some cookbooks that teach you how to prepare delicious low fat meals and learn how to eat better which will help you lose the weight and increase your energy level. The better shape you both are in, the more you will satisfy each other's sexual appetite. Always pay attention to how intensely a man is enjoying his sexual experience with you and how often he wants to do it. The more intense it is and the more he wants to do it the better. Only then can you be really sure that you are truly satisfying him. A woman who can consistently send a man into sexual ecstasy holds a vital key in establishing power and ultimately control over a man.

8

WHEN TO GIVE IT UP

The sooner you give it up the better, and preferably on the first date if it is a guy you really like. In making this statement, I am not talking about high school teenagers. I am talking about mature, adult women. I know that all of the books and articles have told you to hold back because he will want you more and respect you more and you will have a better relationship. Every man knows that women have been taught this. The reality today is, men who have already been put through this process many times before, are tired of it. The fact is a man does not know what your intentions are. He doesn't know whether you plan to make love to him in a month or never at all. Men complain all the time about wasting money, time and effort on women who had no intention of having sex with them or establishing a relationship with them. The older men get, the wiser and more objective they become. The woman who drags out the time in which she is willing to go to bed with a man is viewed as "bull-shiting", and "playing mind games", and therefore can't be trusted. Unless he views you as strictly a friend, or he is so infatuated with you that he will pursue you for the next ten years without having sex, the average man will quickly dump you and move on. Alternatively, he will pursue relationships with other women and the first one to give it up wins.

If you make love to a man on the first date or soon thereafter, the sex issue is out of the way. He trusts you more; he can relax with you more. I have never heard a man complain that his relationship with a woman would have been better if she had put off having sex with him another six months. For me personally I have found that the best and longest lasting relationships I have had with women were the ones in which we made love on the first date or shortly thereafter.

Assuming that you are physically attracted to a man, and you enjoy his company, go ahead and fuck him! Did any of those books or articles tell you exactly how long you should wait? Is it a week? A month? Six months? A year or longer? They never specify this because they know that it will ultimately come down to how you feel, but then what is the difference? If it still comes down to how you feel, and you feel like screwing his brains out on your first or second date then why not?

If you are looking for guarantees, there are none. Just because you make him wait a few months does not mean that the two of you are going to get married and live happily ever after. If that is your objective you are living in a fantasy. We are not living in a world of guarantees. Nothing is promised. Things change. This works both ways. After you have been dating a guy for a few months you may not want him anymore. Whatever happens, you are strong enough to deal with it.

If you are worrying about him respecting you - don't! Any guy who is that immature you should dump immediately. I am assuming, of course, that you are not into pursuing some 19 year old kid who is into gangster rap and is walking around with his underwear sticking out of his pants, and every other word out of his mouth is "bitch" or "whore". If your standards are higher than that then you don't have to worry about the respect issue. Mature men don't think like that. I have never heard a man say that he lost respect for a woman because she made love with him on the first date. Any guy who would say something that stupid and immature you don't want to be around anyway!

Eliminate the tension and ambiguity surrounding whether or not the two of you are going to do the wild thing. The sooner you let him make love to you the better. He will trust you more. Later on there will be lots of little positive games you can play with him to enflame his passions. Review Chapter 2 - Treat Him Inconsistently and Chapter 6 - Kinky Sex.

9

YOUR VOICE

A woman's voice should be soft, seductive and a little exotic. A woman's voice should sound like music to a man's ears. The average woman has no idea how much power she has just by the tone of her voice. Even worse, a lot of women throw all of this power away by trying to talk hard and rough like men. Sounds are important and powerful. Why do you think that people spend billions of dollars every year on music? Most people don't pay attention to the words in songs, and a lot of music does not have any words. It is the effect that the different tones have on people, which stirs their passions. Different tonal combinations can trigger every emotion a person is capable of. Music can make you feel happy or sad, romantic or scared. The advertising industry spends billions of dollars searching for the right tonal combinations to promote their products. The movie industry also devotes a lot of time and money coming up with the right sound effects and music for each scene. The bottom line is, sounds count! Your voice is power!

Brazilian women are considered by many to be the most beautiful women on the planet. Men go crazy when they go to Brazil and date and marry Brazilian women. While it is true that they have beautiful sensuous bodies, take it from me because I have been there many times, it is not just their bodies. It is also their voices. Their voices sound like soft, sweet melodies. I would listen to them for hours barely understanding anything they said, but enjoying every moment of it! Japanese women are also famous for this. Their voices are very soft and feminine.

The problem with most American women is that their voices are too loud and crude. They sound like men. A man does not want his woman to sound like a football player! How can you begin to control a man if you turn him off every time you open your mouth? This is why American men in increasing numbers are turning to foreign women. Men are traveling all over the world to be with women with sweet, innocent, soft voices. They crave this almost as much as they crave great sex. Therefore, always be conscious of how your voice sounds. Keep the tone of your voice low and soft. Even if you have to fake it at first, keep practicing. Listen to how foreign women speak, at least those who have not been in America too long. Rent the video: *Woman On Top* and listen to how the lead actress, Penelope Cruz, speaks and the effects she has on the men in the story. While she is very pretty, there are many far more beautiful women out there, but she knows how to cast a spell with her voice and her charm. While the movie is a romantic comedy it makes a very important point with regards to the potential power that a woman can wield over men just with her voice. When you speak, think soft and feminine!

10

YOUR SMILE

Smile a lot. A smile lights up a woman's face. A woman's smile makes a man feel more relaxed and more comfortable. A radiant smile on a woman can cause a man to drop his guard and be more open to suggestion. When you smile you are sending a very powerful signal to a man, which says that something about him is appealing to you. This will make him feel good about himself and about you.

In addition, people like being around those who are positive and upbeat. Some women are so bitter and filled with so much animosity that they find it difficult to even fake a smile. They are so busy planning and scheming how they are going to get over on the next man who crosses their path that they find it very difficult to smile. A man can almost see the wheels spinning in such a woman's head.

Everyone knows that smiles can be deceiving, nevertheless, a smile still has a tranquilizing affect on people. Some of the most notorious politicians and business leaders have great smiles. If you knew nothing about these people and judged them entirely on the impression you got from watching them on television or meeting them in person, you would probably think that they were decent, honest individuals. Their warm smile would make you inclined to trust them even though they may be capable of committing the greatest forms of evil imaginable. A smile is therefore very powerful.

I once met an elderly gentleman in a department store who was retired. He was from Grenada, and he was very pleasant to talk to. His wife, who was also from Grenada, eventually came and joined the conversation. The moment I saw her I knew why he was so relaxed and pleasant. Despite her age, his wife had a radiant warm smile. She had to be in her sixties, but the warmth that she projected was overpowering. I found myself wishing I had met her when she was younger. From her smile alone, I knew that he was a lucky man.

If you don't want to be perceived as overly negative then smile. You don't have to be giddy or phony. Just a pleasant, warm, friendly smile is all that it takes. A smile does not cost you anything. One of the other amazing things about a nice smile is that it also can have a positive affect on you. When you are smiling, your facial muscles are sending signals to the brain which impacts how you feel. You actually feel happier and more upbeat. You can prove this to yourself. Right now put a big smile on your face and take note of how your feelings start to change.

Likewise, don't be afraid to laugh! Think of funny situations you have been in or funny stories you know about and tell them. If you can get a guy to laugh this will make you more appealing to him than the most expensive perfume. Remember the saying: "Smile and the world will smile with you."

11

YOUR HAIR

While short hair may be cute, long hair is power! Men love long hair on a woman. The longer your hair is the better. A woman with long hair has far greater sex appeal. It may require greater work on your part to maintain it, but it is well worth it if you want to maximize your attractiveness to the man you want or the man you want to keep.

In the story of Samson in the Bible, his strength flowed from his long hair. In other religions, long hair is also associated with power. If you take a plastic comb and run it through your hair quickly several times (your hair must not have grease in it) this will create such an enormous electromagnetic field that you can pick up small pieces of paper with that comb. The point is that there is real tangible power associated with hair. Long hair creates some type of energy field, which attracts the attention of the opposite sex. The longer your hair, the more power you will have over a man!

Wear your hair loose, not tight. A woman who wears her hair tight, looks uptight. Visually, it is more pleasing to a man to look at a woman who has her hair loose. Men also like to run their fingers through a woman's hair, but they can't do this if their woman's hair is as tight as a rope. Therefore, keep your hair loose and inviting.

Avoid using a lot of greasy chemicals on your hair. When a man runs his fingers through your hair, will he end up with a hand full of gooey, greasy chemicals? Men like to feel the natural texture of a woman's hair.

Even though most women are very conscious of how their hair looks, too many women get so caught up in the latest fashion trends that they forget the basics in terms of how to really ignite a man's passions with their hair. The texture of a woman's hair doesn't matter. All that counts is that you stick to the basics, which are: keep your hair long, loose, and free of greasy chemicals. This will enhance your appeal and power over men.

12

BE SPONTANEOUS

Sometimes a man wants to be with his woman on the spur of the moment. Maybe he got a raise, a promotion, or sold his screenplay. Maybe he lost his job or some other misfortune has occurred and you are the one person he wants to be with. You need to go to him during those critical moments. He will always respect you for taking the time to be with him on such occasions. You are sending him a very powerful signal when you do this. You are basically letting him know that you consider him to be important enough to go through the inconvenience involved to see him at the last minute.

If you have kids, it is, of course, a more difficult task to be spontaneous, but you must try. Find a baby-sitter or two who you can count on in emergencies. Make the sacrifice. Be there when he wants you for those special moments. Any woman can say no, or complain about how tired she is, but it is that rare special woman who knows how important this is to him, and will take the time to be with him.

Being spontaneous is what creates magical moments and life long memories. I once dated a woman who I'll call Diana. One night I discovered that one of my favorite singers Astrud Gilberto was performing at a club in New York called S.O.B.'s.

She is the original singer of the song: The Girl From Ipanema. I have always loved that song and I was determined to see her performance. I called Diana up and asked her to go with me. The average woman would spend twenty minutes complaining about it being a weeknight, that she was too tired after working all day, or that she needed more time to plan, or how she had to get up early to go to work. My girl was dressed and ready within an hour. We drank wine by candlelight as we listened to an enchanting musical performance.

Afterwards, since it was a warm summer night, we walked around Greenwich Village in Manhattan for a while. We then started to make out on the hood of my car until a police car started to pull up. We then went to my place and made love for the rest of the night.

The next morning, neither one of us felt like going to work and so we decided not to go. Instead, since it was such a beautiful sunny day we decided to go bike riding. Unfortunately, the only clothes she had was the dress she wore the night before. Instead of driving all the way to her home to get something else to wear she came up with an idea. Diana put on a pair of my boxer shorts, and one of my long sleeve shirts and that is all she wore. It seemed like a wild thing to do, but my shirt was large enough to cover her so I figured what the heck, life is short so why not do something different. I had two bicycles and we rode for hours through Yonkers and Mount Vernon. We found a beautiful lake, which I never knew existed and we bought some food, and camped out by the lake. We hugged and kissed and gave each other massages, as warm breezes blew across the lake. I remember, as I rested my head in her lap while she gently stroked my forehead with her fingers, thinking that this was one of those golden, perfect moments in which I was completely content. There was nothing else in the world I wanted. There was no where else I wanted to be. The whole thing was pure magic for both of us. This enchanting moment in time would not have happened if Diana had not been spontaneous. Most of the things that happen to us in life we forget, but it is those rare spontaneous moments that remain vividly etched into our minds eye.

Be spontaneous!

13

CONVERSATION— DON'T BORE HIM

DON'T TALK TOO MUCH!

If you are the type of woman who can talk 15 minutes straight without a man getting one word in, then you talk too much. You are boring him no matter how much he smiles and nods his head in agreement. I once dated a beautiful Dominican woman who really didn't need me to say anything for her to have a long delightful conversation with me. She could literally talk for forty five minutes to an hour straight without me saying one word or I just made some approving remark such as "ah huh", "really", "interesting". When I was on the telephone with her, I could literally go to the kitchen, get a sandwich, and come back without her noticing. In fact, when I did try to get a word in to actually participate in the conversation she made me feel like I was being rude for interrupting the flow of what she was saying. I tolerated this because she had a very sweet exotic voice, which I loved listening to, a great body, and a good heart. While we had a lot of fun dating, a marriage candidate she was not. I knew that she would drive me crazy if we actually lived together and I had to go through that every day.

If you have something long winded to say, try to limit it to less than thirty seconds and certainly not more than a minute. Try an experiment in which you actually time someone talking for one full minute. You will find that it is a long time for someone else to sit and listen without responding.

Don't bore a man with long, detailed stories about squabbles you got into with other women, family members, neighbors or co-workers. Men in general like to get to the point. They don't like to listen to a whole lot of unnecessary details, especially, "she said this, and I said that" types of discussions. From my experience I have found that women in general prefer to talk about relationships while men tend to prefer to talk about issues. Sports, politics, history, money, business, current events, social issues and of course women, are common topics men like to discuss or debate. Ask yourself this: what percentage of the books you read are romance novels? What percentage of the television programs and movies that you watch are romantic comedies or deal with love triangles? If most of what you read or watch focus on such topics, then what do you really have to discuss with a man, especially one who has a college degree or higher? Don't believe the hype about men not wanting to be with intelligent women unless of course you are interested in some high school drop out with an IQ of fifty hanging out on the corner with his pants drooping down and singing some rap song.

I personally find intelligent women sexy. By intelligent I don't mean only those with advanced degrees, because I have dated women who did not have even have a high school diploma, yet they were very insightful and we had many intriguing discussions which at times turned into fascinating debates. It is a turn on for most men to exchange ideas with a woman about hot news items and different critical issues facing society.

If you don't do it that much already, you should on a regular basis read about political, social and scientific issues in major newspapers and magazines. Don't just watch local news, but also the world news broadcasts as well as the Sunday morning talk shows. You don't have to become an expert on any of these issues, but you could ask interesting questions or get his opinion on some hot political issue. If you know a man you are interested in likes a particular sport then do a little research on that sport. Get a little paperback book on that sport and read it so that you at least know how the game works and then begin watching the sports broadcast on the news, and read the sports section of the newspaper. Again your goal is not to become an expert on the subject, but you want to be able to at least ask interesting questions or make interesting comments about the subject he is interested in. The more you are able to talk about issues that are of interest to him, the more he will enjoy talking to you.

In general, it would be wise to keep discussions about your personal relationship conflicts to a minimum when talking to your man. Furthermore, if you are talking more than fifty percent of the time then you are talking too much. The more time you spend becoming acquainted with various issues, especially those, which are of interest to your man, the more enjoyable conversations you will have.

Ask him lots of questions. Get his advice. Remember that people love to talk and they especially love to give their opinions. Most people don't like listening. Therefore, let him talk. Show genuine interest. He is going to start liking you more and more and he won't even realize why.

Keep your problems to yourself. Everybody is always complaining about something. No one wants to be around someone who is always complaining or who always has problems. Be positive and upbeat even when you are not.

Don't call him too frequently. If he says that he is going to call you then wait until he does. He must respect you! If you are both in the habit of talking everyday then it is okay so long as you are not calling him more often than he is calling you. Now and then skip a day or two and don't call. Make him miss you a little.

Don't talk about your menstrual cycle to or in front of your man. A man in a sense thinks of a woman's vagina as "man candy". He views it as a source of intense ecstasy. Flowers, sunrises, fireworks and all things magical and wonderful he associates with a woman's vagina. By talking about your menstrual cycle you are throwing blood over all of those pleasant images lodged in his mind's eye. Most men won't say anything for fear of seeming immature, but they won't like it. Most women know not to talk about such personal hygiene matters with a man. Nevertheless, many women start to get too relaxed with a man they have been with for a while and start to feel that they can discuss anything with him. Don't make this mistake. Always be ladylike. He will keep you on a pedestal much longer if you do.

Once you eliminate the major things that turn men off, the fewer barriers there will be between you. Fewer barriers there are, the more he will appreciate you, and the more he appreciates you, the more you will succeed in endearing yourself to him. The more you endear yourself to a man the more control you have over him.

14

YOUR POWER OVER MEN

The more feminine you are, the more power you have over a man. Likewise, the more you try to act like a man the less power you have. Too many modern women have been taught that by yelling, screaming, demanding, cursing and ordering, they can get a man to do what they want. Despite what you have seen on television or your liberated friends may have told you, whenever you try to deal with a man like a man you lose! When you step into a man's shoes, you better be prepared to fill them. Men don't like to be yelled at by other men much less by women. When two men are yelling at each other the stage is set for a fight. When a woman is loud and aggressive with a man, she is placing herself in great danger because he can momentarily forget that he is dealing with a woman. Many women have been severely beaten and some killed as a result of jumping in a man's face in a challenging way.

I remember one occasion in which I was a teenager sitting in the back of a movie theater. In the front of the theater an argument broke out. Two women were arguing with a man and a woman sitting in front of them. Suddenly, one of the two women jumped out of her seat yelling and waving her hands in the air challenging the man in front of her to a fight. This huge muscular figure rose from his seat and with one powerful slap the woman went hurdling to the floor. That one blow took all of the fight out of her. She chose to stay on the floor crying rather than face another round with him. I don't advocate violence and most men are not violent, but a woman should never take on a man like a man.

While the average man may not hit you unless you really push him too far, he will definitely lose a lot of respect for you as a woman. He may yell back, he may walk away, he may even give in to your demand or concede that he was wrong, but he will not view you in the same light anymore. You will have become less feminine to him and therefore less precious to him. The less precious you are to a man, the less control you will have over him. In the back of his mind he is thinking: "What a bitch." When he is with his friends he will complain about what a pain in the ass you are. If he meets a more feminine woman he will leave you. If you are married and he can't get out of the marriage easily, he will see other more feminine women. It doesn't matter whether you were right or wrong; if you approach your lover like you are a man you will offend him.

Never try to deal with a man on his turf. Your greatest power lies in your staying on your turf. Stay feminine at all times. To the degree that a man is loud, a woman should be quiet and to the degree that a man is hard a woman must be soft. This does not mean that you are weak, but rather that you are maximizing the influence you were born with. Think of yourself as nylon. Nylon is very soft to the touch, but it is extremely strong. A soft sweet voice, a look of disappointment, and a well placed tear or two can have a far more powerful effect on men than yelling ever will. Furthermore, long after the issue has been resolved he will not have lost any respect for you.

Once I was watching a senate debate on television. A male senator was shouting in a vehement denunciation of some proposed new legislation. Another senator, who was a woman, wanted an opportunity to respond. With a soft voice and a sweet smile she politely asked the senator to yield the floor so that she could speak. At first, he was reluctant, but she kept asking in a soft voice with a warm smile. She made him look like an obnoxious, rude, un-gentleman like bafoon. His expression changed, as he became increasingly embarrassed. He eventually yielded the floor. She held her ground and remained a lady throughout.

On another occasion, I was visiting a friend of mine at his home with his wife. She was very charming and had prepared a delicious meal. I told him that he was a very lucky man to be married to her. He responded by saying: "Oh Yeah, then why don't you take her." He meant it as a joke, but sometimes things don't come out the way they are intended. The bottom line is what he said was very awkward. There was an uncomfortable silence. The average American woman would have been yelling and cursing my friend out for such a remark, but his wife, who was from Trinidad, just sat there silently with her head slightly lowered and a hurt look in her eyes. My friend sprang from his seat in a panic and said "I'm sorry: I didn't mean it." Without saying a word she had exercised the ultimate power a woman has over a man. Her silence spoke volumes. He knew what he said was wrong no matter how unintentional it was. Imagine being able to get a man to admit that he is wrong with just a look! That is real power! That is real control!

This may all seem too subtle and simple, yet it is extremely effective. Men have a soft spot for women, which they don't have for men. Men don't like to see a woman crying or to see a woman in pain. Every man has a mother. Deep down he is as protective of all women as he is of his own mother. A woman is also like a delicate flower, which is every man's duty to protect even at the expense of his own life. From a biological level, without women the human race dies. Therefore, innately, men know that they have to protect and care for women. The problem is that over the years modern women have been taught to act like men. The harder women try to be like men, the less respect men have for them as women. This is why men don't give up their seats to women. Why should they if most of the women around them are really men inside female bodies? Men give up their seats and extend other courtesies to ladies, not female impersonators! If you think wearing a skirt, carrying a purse, and wearing a lot of makeup is all that it takes to be a lady, think again. What is on the inside of you is far more important in defining you as a lady than what is on the outside.

You can talk to a man about almost any problem, so long as you stay lady like as you do it. Keep your voice soft. Never demand, or order, instead only question and make suggestions. Allow your expressions to convey any disappointment you may have more so than your words. It is okay for a lady to show her emotions to a man provided that she does it in a non-threatening way. A lady does not have to be aggressive to get a man to do what she wants. A lady only has to suggest what she would like and her man will be eager to get whatever she needs to make her happy. By appealing to a man's emotions you reactivate the innate affections and vulnerability he has for all women. He will want to appease you and to do everything to avoid hurting you. Think of yourself as a beautiful, delicate, rare flower, which needs to be protected and cared for. A man can not appeal to another man in this way, only a woman can. Is this being manipulative? Yes, of course it is, but it is the type of manipulation that men don't mind because it reminds and reinforces the fact that he is a man and you are a lady! A woman defines a man's purpose for being. Men are lost souls without women. They need someone to provide for and protect. This is an innate impulse in men, which is still there despite all of the problems that exist between the sexes in modern societies. A lady knows this and knows that all she has to really do is point the way and her man will struggle to get or do whatever she wants.

Some men are so bitter and hardened that they are not ready to deal with a lady yet in their lives. Don't keep hitting your head against a wall over such men. A lady does not have to stress herself out over any man. If you are dealing with such a man, you should dump him and establish a relationship with someone who is less negative and is very responsive to a woman who acts like a lady.

Never listen to anyone who advises you to act like a man. When you act like a man you will be treated like a man. When you act like a lady you maximize your power over men.

15

WHAT TURNS GUYS OFF

COSMETICS

When it comes to cosmetics, natural is better. The most beautiful women I have ever seen wore little to no make up. So long as you are clean, have a nice smile, and a sweet personality that is enough for most men.

Many cosmetics aren't tested for their long-term side effects. There are many different cosmetic ingredients that are known to cause cancer. There is a long list of other side effects from cosmetics. Therefore, before kissing, remove lipstick and facial makeup. If the two of you are tongue kissing, that means that the both of you are swallowing lipstick and other chemicals which will circulate throughout the organs of your body increasing your risk of one terrible disease or another. If you must use cosmetics, go to a good health food store and see what natural cosmetics they have.

Trust me. I'm a guy. I know what really beautiful women look like. Think of the top female vocalists, models and actresses out there. They mean nothing to me, because I have dated far more beautiful women. I am talking about devastatingly gorgeous women who make men stop in their tracks drooling at the mouth. Men with money and men who travel around the world know what I am talking about. My point is, I know what extraordinarily beautiful women look like and one of the traits they have in common is that they wear little to no makeup! Natural beauty is far more powerful! You don't need all of that makeup! Keep it simple.

PERFUME

Make sure that you are wearing perfumes that he really likes. Take him shopping with you or get some perfume samples and ask him which ones he likes best on you. By doing this you can know for sure that he likes the scent you are wearing.

In light of what I have said about cosmetics in general, a dermatologist once told me to only apply colognes to my clothing and not to my skin. This is something you should also consider doing.

GUM

Don't chew gum. It is not lady like. It turns guys off very fast. Guys find it obnoxious looking at a woman chewing gum.

SPITTING

Don't spit. It is crude for a woman to do this.

CURSING

Don't curse in front of your man. It is extremely unladylike. The one exception of course is when you are deliberately talking dirty to him in intimate situations to heighten his arousal.

BAD BREATH

As hard as many women work at keeping themselves clean, it is amazing how many don't pay enough attention to their breath. Make sure that your breath really smells good before kissing and before sex. If you are not sure, ask him in a non-intimate moment, if your breath could be improved. Tell him that you read a book that encouraged couples to engage in open, frank, communications. Some people do have more serious problems causing bad breath and they should seek medical help.

LADIES ROOM

Never say in front of a man that you have to go "pee." Men find women who talk like this to be disgusting, even though they might smile pleasantly as if it didn't matter. Just like women, guys compare notes when they get together. No guy likes a woman who acts or talks like a pig. Say you have to go to the ladies room, or to powder your nose, or anything other than words like "pee" or "urinate." Such words should not be a part of a woman's vocabulary, at least not in the presence of men.

SKIRTS & DRESSES

Men like seeing other women in short dresses, but not the woman they are dating! If you are wearing a short dress and other guys are staring at you or worst, making inappropriate comments, this could lead to a fight. Therefore, wear dresses often, but keep them no more than slightly above your knees or a little longer. Even if you are going to a club to meet guys, don't wear a short dress. Many decent men won't bother with you because you are like a walking neon sign. They would be too afraid that you would just reject them. They will think that you are looking for some "playboy type". It is unlikely, but you may actually get that smooth talking "playboy" to approach you, but keep in mind that those types have lots of other options besides you. If you really want to run in the "fast lane", be prepared to pay the price! Therefore, you would do best to dress modestly, elegantly, and very ladylike.

Wear soft feminine colors. Yellow or pink on a woman personally drives me crazy. Avoid red. It is too loud and makes you look like a slut.

SKINTIGHT PANTS & JEANS

A woman walking down the street in a pair of jeans that are so tight that they show every curve in her butt and thighs, as she shakes and jiggles tantalizing every man who spots her, is great for guys in general, but not for the guy she is with. A man does not want his woman drawing all of that type of attention to herself. A man wants his woman to dress like a lady. He wants her to look elegant, not like a potential hooker. It is okay to be cute and sexy, but not loud and obnoxious about it. Always dress ladylike.

YOUR BODY

Get in shape. Nothing kills a man's desire for you quicker than being out of shape. If you are overweight, find a diet plan and an exercise routine that works for you. There are a lot of them. If you are slender, you should still go to the gym to tone up your muscles. A nicely toned body is very sensual. Find a gym located near your job. It may be a whole lot easier to go to the gym right after work than to go home first and then try to motivate yourself to go back out and go to a gym near your home.

After a pregnancy and you get your strength back, you must make it a priority to get rid of all of the extra weight that you put on. If you are married, your husband has waited a long time to make love to you. The quicker you can get back to the figure you were before, the happier he will be. A lot of marriage problems occur as a result of a woman losing some of her sex appeal as a result of her gaining the extra weight from pregnancy, but not taking it off.

Hire a good physical fitness instructor at your gym. He or she will get you into a routine that fits your physical condition. They will show you how to use the equipment, how to pace yourself, what exercises you need and probably recommend a diet that's right for you. The wonderful thing about exercising is that once you get into a routine, it takes on a life of its own. You actually look forward to exercising. If you use an instructor for at least nine months you will feel better, look better, and be more attractive to your man.

Find some type of sport or other physical activity you

enjoy doing. Tennis, volleyball, fencing, swimming, belly dancing, or bicycling are some of the types of activities you should also consider doing on a weekly basis to get some additional exercise. If you are having fun with a particular activity then you will do it more often and burn off the unwanted fat in the process.

Before you eat anything else during the day, eat some fruits, chew on some carrots, eat salads, drink fruit and vegetable juices first. If you consume these things first you will have less cravings and less room for the bad things you want to eat.

Don't eat late at night. Try to eat before 8 p.m. If you eat late at night your body will process the food slower.

As you are working to tone up, don't set your goal to look like one of those sickly looking, skinny models. Men like women who have some meat on their butts and thighs. The skin and bones look may be the fashion industry's idea of beauty, but it is not what most men consider to be sexy. I have often fantasized what would happen if there was a beauty contest judged by ordinary men in which skinny American models had to compete against shapely Brazilian or East European women. I predict that the American models would be put to shame. There is a music video entitled: "I Like Butt", which spells out exactly what men like to see in terms of a woman's figure. Therefore get in shape, but don't shoot for the skinny look.

BREAST IMPLANTS AND COSMETIC SURGERY

Do not deform yourself with breast implants or cosmetic surgery. Large breasts on a woman do have a certain appeal to men, but so do her ass, thighs, clothes, hairstyle, smile and most of all her personality. How well a woman juggles all of these other variables is where the art and magic of being a woman comes in. You don't need artificial breast implants to attract or satisfy a man. I have never heard a man complain that he didn't have a good time in bed with a woman because her breasts were too small. Brazilian women, Japanese women, and French women are not known for having large breasts, yet men fantasize about these women. You don't have to mutilate yourself to have sex appeal. A real woman uses the equipment she was born with to cast her spell over men. Besides men find breast implants revolting to look at and disgusting to touch. What kind of weird guy would want to put his hand or mouth on some artificial, toxic, chemical concoction? They may be great to look at from a distance while you have your clothes on, but when he actually feels them and realizes what you have done to yourself, he is repulsed. In addition, he knows that you are suffering from a severe self-esteem problem. A man wants a woman with her natural soft breasts, whatever size they are.

The same is true for cosmetic surgery. I have been stunned, as I have listened to women express their desire to cut up their nose, lips or other parts of their body to become more beautiful. I would go through great pains trying to convince these women that there was nothing wrong with how they looked and I meant it. These were attractive women who some magazine or television commercial must have convinced them that the way their nose or other part of their body looked, was below the standards of someone's concept of beauty.

While cosmetic surgery may have a role for those who were disfigured as a result of an accident or illness, anything beyond that is totally unnecessary.

The more surgeries you have, and the more artificial things you put onto or into your body, the greater your risk for breast cancer, and a long list of other diseases. You may not want to think about such things now, but you will later when you are laid up in a hospital with some disease eating away at you and you are on constant medication just to cope with the pain. Life is short enough, why increase your risk of going through such a nightmare? Therefore stay away from breast implants, and cosmetic surgery.

If you are really that serious about enhancing your sex appeal, go to the gym regularly and lose that weight you have been planning to lose. Change your eating habits so that you are consuming less salty, greasy foods. Get rid of all of those layers of cosmetics so that when a man kisses you he is not taking in a whole chemical factory. If you have a loud voice and an aggressive, independent personality, then make your voice softer and your personality less aggressive and independent. Study the art of lovemaking and never allow sex with you to become boring. Read and reread *The Secrets*. If you take these steps you won't have to worry about your sex appeal!

YOUR MENSTRUAL CYCLE

Don't ask a man to have intercourse with you while you are menstruating. Most women know not to do this, but there are some who seem to think that there is nothing wrong with it. Men don't like to do this. I personally know of only one guy who said it didn't matter to him. For the rest of us it does matter. Some women even seem to think that it is funny to have sex with a man and not tell him that she is menstruating. If you do this, he will think of you as a pig and lose respect for you and probably not want to deal with you anymore because you are unpredictable and not trustworthy.

Because a woman has been dealing with her menstrual cycle since she was a teenager, it is no big deal for her, but a man does not want to associate or think about blood in reference to the source of his ultimate pleasure - your vagina! Always be a lady. Wait until your cycle is finished and then fuck him as much as you want.

ASSURING HIM YOU'RE CLEAN

Don't go to the bathroom and urinate and then jump into bed expecting him to give you oral sex. The reason is obvious. Rinsing yourself at the sink is not good enough. How does he know that you are not just washing your hands? You must get into the shower and wash yourself. If he hears the shower, he knows that you are washing yourself thoroughly and therefore he will be more receptive to your request for oral sex.

YOUR BREATH AFTER ORAL SEX

When you give a man a blowjob, don't expect him to kiss you right afterwards. Even if you rinse your mouth out, there will still be a strong smell. Don't breathe directly in his face either for the same reason.

FORGIVING, BUT NOT FORGETTING

Probably the number one thing that men complain about with regards to women is the fact that they always bring up past mistakes or problems. Once a situation is over and you have said that you forgive him, that is it! Let it go! Never mention it again. The more you keep bringing up something that happened in the past, the more you will drive a wedge between you and him. You are teaching him not to trust you. What you are telling him in effect is that what he thought was over and forgiven was never really over or forgiven. In some ways men are like children in that when children have a problem, they fight, but once the fight is over all is forgiven. Five minutes later they are playing together, and whatever happened is quickly forgotten. Men are the same way. A man can have a verbal or physical fight one week with another man and the following week the two of them could be watching football and drinking beers together. For most men, once a problem is over it is over!

Too many women feel that for the rest of their lives, they have to hold on to the memory of something bad that their man did. They allow it to sit inside them festering, waiting for opportunities to remind their man of what he did.

I met a charming Brazilian woman on a flight to Rio De Janeiro. Her name was Regina. She had been married 24 years and she told me that she was more in love with her husband than ever. I asked her what was the secret to the success of their marriage, and to my amazement, the first thing she said was that when she forgave her husband about something she really forgave him. She never mentioned it again. She also noted that when she was wrong she was willing to admit it and ask his forgiveness. I found speaking with her to be very inspiring.

Therefore, if you forgive him then it is over, never to be mentioned again. If you can't forgive him, then leave him. If he keeps doing the same thing and it is something you consider to be very serious such as excessive gambling or drinking and you have been unable to help him to correct the problem through counseling or other means, then leave him.

HIS PAST RELATIONSHIPS

Don't ask a man, especially one you recently met, about his past relationships with other women. This is none of your business. His past relationships have nothing to do with his current relationship with you. Judge him based on how he treats you. Men consider such inquiries to be prying. They also view such women as superficial, because they are more concerned with the past than the present.

Too many women have an overwhelming need to collect intelligence on a man they are interested in. The more he reveals, the better able she is to size him up and draw a conclusion, or so they thinks. Most men who have answered such inquiries eventually learned that no matter what they said they would lose. Whether he broke it off with his last girlfriend or she broke it off with him, to the woman he is telling this to, he is still the bad guy or something must be wrong with him, so she must probe deeper to uncover the truth. I hate to tell you this, but a woman's intuition is not 100%. If it was, then why is the divorce rate so high in this country? Given the fact that women ultimately are the ones who choose the men they are willing to be with, a lot of women are obviously choosing the wrong men. Therefore, don't try to create a psychological profile on a man based on his past relationships. It is rude, inaccurate and unnecessary. Focus on the man right in front of you.

I HAVE TWO KIDS

When you first meet a man you are interested in, don't let the first words out of your mouth be a confession about how many kids you have. I know that a lot of women do this to protect themselves. They want the guy to know up front what the situation is. Unfortunately, this is the wrong logic. Why throw a damper on things before they have a chance to warm up. Without a doubt, for a single man without kids, a woman with kids would require a lot more patience on his part. There will be many times that he will want to see you, but he won't be able to because of your kids. Some of your dates will involve taking your kids along. While challenges like these are real and do run through a man's head, they are not insurmountable, especially if you get him to really like you first. Therefore, let him get to know you first! Go out on dates, let him make love to you. Later you can ease him into more details about your family life. Give yourself time to cast your spells on him.

A man will respect you more and enjoy your company more if you don't do those things which turns him off.

16

THE OTHER WOMAN

Too many women drive their men crazy with constant accusations about them seeing other women. A lot of women become a detective when they are in a relationship with a man. They are constantly conducting inspections and interrogations to determine if their man is seeing another woman. They snoop around his apartment looking for another woman's hair, bobby pins, jewelry or anything else that can prove that another female had been there. They constantly ask him questions about his whereabouts, probing for inconsistencies. While a little jealousy is cute and expected, the fanatical jealousy which too many women are obsessed with, is overkill and will destroy a relationship quicker than boring sex.

One woman I dated found a picture of another woman in my home. It was just a photograph of a woman sitting on a rock. The picture was about five years old and the person in the photo was never more than a friend whom I hadn't spoke to in years. Nevertheless, this one insignificant picture was enough for her to drag me into a big argument. We broke up after this incident and became just good friends later on. Millions of men are constantly put through the same thing. Relationships breakup all the time over this nonsense.

Instead of driving yourself crazy worrying about whether he is seeing another woman, focus on making yourself more desirable and precious to him by following the advice given in *The Secrets*. Lose the weight and tone your body up to maximize your physical attraction. Follow the guidelines for improving your sexual performance. Play positive mind-games with him as outlined. Follow the other suggestions which have been given and you will have him desiring you more and more.

Reality check time. Do a lot of men see or desire to see other women on the side? Of course they do. Keep in mind that men are bombarded with sex seven days a week. When a man walks down the street he sees women wearing tight fitting jeans, short dresses, and tight blouses, shaking and jiggling as they strut past him. Whenever he turns on the television, watches a video, opens a magazine, or even reads a newspaper he sees all types of gorgeous women posing, jiggling, and doing everything possible to arouse him sexually. Sex does sell. Therefore, there is no mystery as to why men are always thinking about sex. Your fellow women have saturated the atmosphere with sexually charged energy!

Some cultures became so concerned with the disruptive potential of women using their bodies to constantly arouse men that they set up all types of severe dress codes to limit their ability to do this. Certain Islamic sects don't allow women to expose any part of their body in public. Modern women are still required to wear bras. I saw a documentary on an experiment that took place in Brazil. A woman was paid to live 24 hours a day in a glass apartment in full public view. When she took a shower or undressed at any time her naked body was in full view of everyone. Within a few days the men rioted trying to get to her. The police had they're hands full. Needless to say the experiment with the woman was discontinued.

Women often get upset when the man they are with turns to glance at some woman giggling past them in some skintight outfit. But instead of getting mad with the man, she should be upset with the woman for dressing in a way that sends out such strong sexual signals. Sex is one of the most powerful driving forces in nature and women deliberately flaunt themselves in front men which is like waving a match around a ton of dynamite. All women of course don't do this, but a lot of them do. Amazingly, a lot of parents allow their young teenage daughters to dress in tight jeans, short blouses with their belly exposed, and dress in other ways totally inappropriate for young teenage girls. I wonder at times, what is going through the minds of some of these parents. Do they really want teenage boys and men staring at their 15-year-old daughter's butt twitching as she walks down the street?

Because men are constantly being tempted, when the opportunity presents itself, a lot of men will give into temptation. You may consider this to be irresponsible, but his motivations are more biological than psychological. The primary function of sex is reproduction not pleasure. Sex was made pleasurable to encourage reproduction. In nature, species have sex only for reproduction. During the mating season that is the only time that most species have sex. In some traditional cultures they also believe in having sex only during certain cycles. My point is that women who do provocative things in public are triggering powerful biological responses in men. In fact, the argument could be made that men are constantly being subjected to mental cruelty since they can not act on their impulses once they have been aroused. Therefore, don't put all of the blame on the men for seeing other women on the side.

There are at least three powerful things you can do with regards to your man and the other woman.

1. DON'T WORRY ABOUT IT

Don't try to find anything and ignore what you do find. Just accept that during the course of a long-term relationship your man may see another woman at some point. It could be because he is bored with you sexually. It could be because he just has a desire for variety. It could be because he met someone who had that certain look which got to him and she was willing. You should also keep this in mind: the other woman has also saved many relationships and marriages. A man might have loved his wife, but been bored with her in bed. In this situation he saw himself as having two choices: a). Get a divorce or b). See another woman on the side who can gratify him sexually. So long as the wife didn't find out, the marriage was saved. Just because he sees another woman, it does not mean that he no longer loves you or that he wants to leave you.

One woman I spoke to had been married many years with her husband and had four children with him. She told me that for years her female friends would come to her and tell her about her husband cheating on her with different women. She said that she just ignored them because her husband worked very hard and he always brought home the money. Her husband was a bus driver and I spoke to him about his marriage. He told me that women hit on him all the time when he was driving a bus. For years he fooled around, but he eventually lost all interest in other women and just wanted to be with his wife. This couple is still together and they recently bought a new home. The easiest thing for his wife to have done would have been to get a divorce from her husband, but then she would have had to raise her children largely by herself, she wouldn't have gotten that much money for child support, and because she was in her forties, very overweight, and had four children, she would have had a hard time getting another man in her life. She correctly perceived that what her husband was doing did not mean that he didn't love her or that he wanted to leave. She ignored it and kept her marriage and family together.

Keep in mind that until a few hundred years ago, polygamy was accepted and legal over most of world. Polygamy is a marriage system in which a man can legally have several wives. Even today, polygamy is still practiced in many parts of the world. It seems that these cultures understood a man's natural urges and incorporated them into their societies. Who's to say whether the natural order of things for the human species is for males to have multiple female mates or just one? Every species has it's own unique mating pattern. In some species the male and female mate for life. In some, the male has multiple females. In some species such as certain spiders, the female tries to eat the male after he mates with her. If you consider the history of males and females, men tend to have an innate desire to have multiple women. Laws which prohibit polygamy, coupled with the effort to make men feel guilty about being with or desiring to be with other women may be going against the grain of nature. One of the reasons why prostitution is a multi-billion dollar industry is because men need that sexual outlet. It is not just single guys who use the services of call girls, but a lot of married men also. Prostitution is a natural compromise between a man's sexual impulses and the cultural restrictions, which have been imposed on him. When you couple a man's natural sexual urges with the massive sexual stimuli, which saturates our modern society, you can see that there are powerful forces driving him sexually.

I am not suggesting that you have to join some religious group, which allows polygamy, but that you are more under-standing with regards to why a man might see another woman. I should also point out that most, if not all men, can be perfectly content with one woman. I have spoken to many men who have been married ten years or more who told me that they never slept with another woman since they were married. Of the men I spoke to, this was not due to any religious convictions, but rather they were just content and very happy with their wives. Don't worry about the other woman; worry instead about keeping your man happy.

2. FUCK HIM ALOT

Give him so much hot sex that he is too satisfied and worn out to deal with other women. See Chapter 7 Sex With You - How To Measure His Excitement. This will give you an idea of how much he really enjoys making love to you. Once you are confident that he is really enjoying you sexually, then all you have to do is give him enough to keep him so preoccupied with you that he won't have the desire or the energy to deal with another woman.

3. CREATE MAGIC

Once you are able to create a feeling of magic in him, you got him! It will cool any burning desires he has to see another woman. If a smile forms on his face when he thinks about you, then you have enchanted him. You have successfully cast your magical spell over him. How do you create magic? You create it by being sweet, by smiling, by being innocent, by being spontaneous, by speaking in a soft feminine voice, by touching him in an affectionate way, by doing little things for him that most modern women won't do, by cooking great dishes for him, and by creating special magical moments. You create magic by doing all of the things described in *The Secrets*. Of the ones listed, creating magical moments is one of the most important yet often neglected by women, especially those who have been in a relationship with a particular man for long time. Review Chapter 12 on being spontaneous.

When a man thinks of a woman, his mind flashes back to a few special moments with her that set his heart aglow and brings a smile to his face. The more of those moments that he has with you, the greater the magical spell you will have cast over him and the more control you will have. Often magical moments just happen, but magical moments can also be planned for. It could be something as simple sitting on a beach at night under a bright full moon, sipping champagne. You don't need to spend a lot of money to create magical moments. The most important thing is that you do something different from the norm. For example, get him to agree to take a day off from work in the middle of the week and the two of you just do something fun together. You could go to a museum, aquarium or amusement park. Later take him to a professional masseur and you treat the both of you to a massage. End the day with dinner and hot sex. Twenty years in the future he will still remember your special day together. The most important ingredient in creating magical moments is that it is something very different from what the two of you normally do. When you put your mind to it, there are all sorts of things that you can come up with. The only thing more powerful than his sexual urge is that magical glow that he feels when he thinks of you. Some might call it love, but in reality it is a feeling that is different yet compliments love. There are many people who think that they are in love, but don't have that warm enchanted feeling. Love can turn to hate in a heartbeat, but that magical feeling is far more understanding, durable and mellow. Older couples understand this. They may use the term "love" to describe their feelings for each other, but they know that what they have is far more special. Think of love as fire and magic as the red-hot glowing amber. The amber is hotter and lasts longer than the fire. Think of love as excitement and magic as contentment. Therefore stop worrying about the other woman, if there is one. Instead, focus on making him so satisfied and enchanted with you that you quench his thirst for anyone else. Create magic!

17

MEN TO AVOID

MEN WHO ARE ADDICTED

Stay away from alcoholics, drug addicts and gamblers. Such men are obviously extremely unstable. Despite whatever sex appeal or charm he may have, this type of man will cause you more harm than good. If you insist on being with such a person, don't blame *The Secrets* for what happens, you have only yourself to blame.

ABUSIVE TYPES

Stay away from men who hit you, routinely yell at you or curse at you. Too many women seem to enjoy being put in their place by such men, but over the long run they get tired of the abuse and crave a more even-tempered man who is a real gentleman. They wish that they had given that teacher, plumber, or account-ant who liked them, a second chance. A man who has no problem with routinely calling you a bitch or slapping you in the face, does not respect you. If you pursue or stay with these kinds of men you will end up in the hospital or dead or you will end up killing him. If kids are involved, then the situation will of course be much worst. You must emotionally and physically pull away from such men. There are literally millions of men out there who can satisfy your every sexual desire and give you the happiness and respect you deserve.

RICH PLAYBOYS

Keep in mind that the sexier the guy and the more money he has, the more options he has in terms of women. You may be able to get such a man in bed, but how long can you keep him there? If you follow the guidelines in *The Secrets* you will be way ahead of the others. Remember though that a lot of women are after men like this, so you have to put extra effort in keeping him focused on you. Many women would do much better with average looking men with average careers and then molding them into what they want. A woman who has established control over a man by following the guidelines listed here would have no problem motivating a man to go to the gym regularly and pumping some iron or taking a second job to make more money. Once a man considers you to be precious because of all of the things you do for him as described here, he will find a way to do what is necessary to make you happy. Lots of average men have become multi-millionaires with the right women inspiring them. If you really want a rich "playboy", then go for it, but just be prepared for the additional challenges that this will present. At least consider the millions of average guys out there and molding them into what you want.

MEN WHO ARE NOT INTERESTED IN YOU

Too many women waste a lot of time and effort on men who are clearly not interested in them. They eventually get frustrated and start to feel that all men are no good. You know when a man is not that interested in you. He has a "I couldn't careless" attitude towards you. He can go days or weeks without calling you or returning your phone call. He can easily go days, weeks or even months without having sex with you. He is not responsive to your needs and desires. In extreme cases, he has no problem with routinely yelling and cursing at you. He may have a great body, he may fuck you better than any other guy you have ever had, but he is not right for you. He will lead you down an endless path of pain and frustration. If he treats you inconsistently, as mentioned earlier in Chapter 2, you will mis-interpret his signals and actually believe that you are in love with him. When this happens you are really in trouble! The two of you will eventually separate, but it will be a long aggravating process, with the final breakup being very traumatic for you. Sure, if you apply what you have learned in *The Secrets* you can have almost any man, but the path is a much longer and winding one when you insist on pursuing or maintaining a relationship with a man who is not interested in you.

Never get hung up over why a man is not interested in you. That is not your business, especially if you are not married to this person. You probably don't want to know anyway. Think back to when you were in a club and guys who you had no interest in came up to you and started talking to you or asked you to dance. You didn't want to tell them that they were too fat, too short or dressed like a geek. You hoped that they would just go away quietly before you said something to really hurt their feelings. Likewise, if a guy is giving you all types of strong negative signals, just accept it and move on, because there are plenty of guys out there who would be very happy in a relationship with you.

One of the keys to controlling a man therefore is to focus your energies on men who already like you. It is far easier to cast your spells on men who are already willing subjects. The ones who occasionally say dumb things as they try to impress you, or are always calling you, or are always eager to take you out, or are always hungry to make love to you, those are the ones you should focus your efforts on. It is easy for women to view such men as boring and not a challenge, but these men are the ones who would give you the world. They are your potential lifelong marriage partners. If you apply what you learned in *The Secrets* to such men they will be putty in your hands. Too many women pass up potentially beautiful relationships with men, simply because these men already like them and are too easy. Never underestimate what any properly motivated man is capable of doing or becoming.

Therefore, avoid guys who are clearly not interested in you and focus your efforts on the ones who are.

OVERLY JEALOUS TYPES

While a little jealousy may be cute, too much is destructive. Some men are obsessively jealous when it comes to their girl-friend or wife. Men like this will constantly accuse you of doing something with another man. You will be always arguing with him and defending yourself. There is nothing cute or funny about this type of man. Not only will he send your blood pressure up, he can and eventually will physically hurt you when he goes into one of his wild rampages accusing you of fooling around. Men like this can kill you. If you are seeing someone on the side, and if this type of man catches you, you can end up in the hospital or the cemetery. Too many women are drawn to men like this and they suffer the consequences. Once again, a little jealousy now and then is normal for any man, but the men who are obsessively jealous and accuse you of something on a regular basis, are very dangerous to your emotional and physical well being. Therefore, stay away from the overly jealous types.

Always concentrate your efforts on men who are not addicted to something, who are positive, even tempered, and are already infatuated with you.

18

DON'T POISON
THE ATMOSPHERE

Don't waste time playing mind-games with guys you are not interested in. For example, if a man asks you for your number, why waste time and play with his head by giving him a wrong number? If you don't want to give him your phone number, then tell him you have a boyfriend. Likewise, why go out on a date with a man if you are 100% certain that you are never going to fuck him? Why go to a man's home alone, at night if you know for certain that you don't want to have sex with him? Mind-games are fine if they are designed to get or keep the man you want. Anything else is a waste of your time and his time and money. Every man has stories of women who caused him to waste a lot of time and spend a lot of money, but they still didn't give it up. Don't try to hide behind the notion that those were just friendship dates. If you were just friends, then you should have insisted on going Dutch.

While you may be using these men to boost your ego, or to just get out of the house until your mister right comes along, you are doing harm to him and to yourself. Your rejects are another women's lucky catch. The same applies to the man you ultimately decide you want. He has had the same games played on him and that baggage is being brought into the relationship with you. He has become hardened. He has placed a defensive shell around himself to protect his feelings. He will be reluctant to let you get too close to his heart. Since he has experienced women who have lied to him by giving him false numbers and played with him in all sorts of ways, he feels that most women are manipulative and not trustworthy. While you are viewing him as a potential mate, he is viewing you as a piece of ass. This is why the expression "getting over" is often used in reference to a man getting a woman in bed. Men encounter so much unpredictability and manipulation when it comes to "modern" women, that encounters with women are often reduced to whether or not he was able to get sex and with the least amount of time, money and effort.

Men are traveling in droves all over the world to find women who are more interested in finding decent stable men than playing mind-games. I am talking about men who are lawyers, doctors, bankers, real estate developers, authors, public speakers, entertainers, and others. Increasingly they are looking to find wives in countries where the women can't afford the books and magazines that fill their heads with all sorts of negative thoughts about men. These women are in essence: purer, sweeter and a breath of fresh air from all of the mind-games and unpredictability that American women put them through. Men talk about the problem with modern women all the time. You may be sneering at all of this, but the fact remains, that the atmosphere between men and women in modern western societies like America has been poisoned by a lot of unnecessary, unproductive mind-games. Without a doubt men have their flaws too, but this book is about what you women should consider doing differently.

Playing nasty manipulative games with men you don't want, over time becomes a part of your personality, and men can sense this. Just as you can sense flaws in a man, men can sense the same thing in you. While they still might want to fuck you, and perhaps have a few laughs with you, they sense what you are capable of and so they keep an emotional distance between the two of you, because you potentially could turn on them at any moment. Therefore, play positive mind games such as those suggested in this book, but only directed at the men you want! Don't poison the atmosphere for other women and yourself by playing juvenile mind games on men you are not interested in.

19

LIMIT WHAT YOU SAY

Some women feel that just because they are angry, they are entitled to say every four-letter word they can think of. They will say the nastiest, foulest things imaginable. They will think of their lover's greatest flaws or most embarrassing moments and use them to rip deeply into his heart and soul. Do you really think that after breaking him down in this manner that the two of you can kiss and make up and all will be forgiven? Once you cross the line in terms of what you say, there is no going back. You may even stay together afterwards, but the relationship will never be the same. Even worse, the time will come when you are at one of your lowest points in life as a result of being financially devastated, or having a serious health problem, or you are dealing with some other crisis. When you are in fact the most vulnerable and need him the most, this is when he will remember those horrible things you said. Therefore, always be conscious of what you are saying when you are angry and make sure you are not going too far.

20

BE TRUSTWORTHY

When a man is considering getting serious with a woman, especially when it comes to marriage, one of the critical issues for him is: can he trust this person? Can he share his victories and defeats, triumphs and failures? Can he share his most guarded secrets with her? Can he afford to risk tying his financial future with her? Will she run away or divorce him at the first sign of trouble? Can she really hang in there for the long haul by his side no matter what obstacles are encountered?

When I am with my male friends, we talk about this all the time. Given the fact that increasingly marriages don't last, and men can be financially ruined as a result of divorce proceedings, most men are very concerned about how much they can trust a woman. Ordinary men have to worry about this just as much as rich men do. If a man who is worth $20 million has to give up half in a divorce settlement, he may not like it, but he is not going to have to worry about keeping up the mortgage payment or figuring out where his next meal is going to come from. A man making $30,000 has a lot more to worry about if he has to give up half of his income to his former wife.

Men look for little clues to see if they can trust you. Is your bookshelf filled with books dealing with how men are no good? Are you always watching movies and television broadcasts that portray men in a negative light? Do you have a dozen different woman's magazines on your coffee table? You may not realize it, but many men do periodically stop and read those women's magazines and know the type of advice they are giving you.

Worst of all, do you gossip with your friends about personal matters of other men? If your circle of female friends reveal embarrassing, awkward little details about their men to you, he will assume that you are probably also sharing personal information about him. In either case, you can't be trusted. Nobody wants their dirty laundry aired in public. Therefore avoid participating in such gossip. Make it a part of your personality to respect the privacy of others.

Of course there are times when a girlfriend is crying in your arms and telling you all types of terrible things about her boyfriend or husband. That is different from what some women do, which is to divulge personal tidbits about their men in almost every conversation they have. Such women live for this type of daily gossip. Once again I am speaking from experience. I have had female friends who would stun me with the types of things that their girlfriends would tell about their boyfriends and husbands. I wasn't as shocked by what the men supposedly did, as I was by the fact that their trusted companions revealed such things to their girlfriends. How much do you think I could trust the women I was with who would tell me such things? Therefore, avoid gossiping too much. At the very least don't let your man know that gossiping with your friends is your favorite pastime. Definitely don't tell him about what your girlfriends said about their men. If you do, he will only assume that you are doing the same and therefore you can't be trusted.

BE UNDERSTANDING

Be understanding about whatever he reveals to you. When your man was at his lowest point, how did you react? Maybe he got burnt in the stock market, couldn't close a big deal, or got laid off. What was your reaction to the news? You can't control a man if he doesn't trust you with his setbacks and personal weaknesses.

When he has bad news, try to lift his spirits. Make suggestions as to what he might try in order to correct the problem or how he might avoid making the same mistake again. Even if you don't have any ideas, let him know that you will be by his side no matter what. Cook him a nice meal, give him a massage, fuck his brains out and then take a bath together by candlelight with soft music playing. You will have him eating out of your hands. He will begin to trust you more than any other woman he has been with. Few women would treat him so well when he was feeling so low and therefore you are very special.

Creating this type of trust is very critical. Life is full of ups and downs. Even men of great wealth have lost everything. Every man is conscious of this and deep down is afraid of this happening to him. No man wants to be in a position in which he can't provide for his beloved wife and family, or is facing foreclosure on their home or has to file bankruptcy, or worst. This is the real world. Things happen. A man wants to commit to a woman who will truly be at his side as the wedding vows command: "Til death do you part". It is easy for a man with some money to have a beautiful young woman around while times are good, but if times were to change how long can he count on her to she stick around? When a man is thinking about a serious commitment to a woman, especially marriage, he has to know that she will be there for him no matter what challenges he has to face.

When he is sick, drop everything to be at his side taking care of him. Even if he just has the flu and has to stay home for a few days. Go to his home and cook for him. Go shopping for him. Take his temperature. Put the back of your hand on his forehead to see if it is hot. Even if you don't know what you are doing it will remind him of what his mother use to do when he was a child and he was sick. In terms of building trust, being by someone's side when they are sick is very powerful. They will always remember that you were there for them when they were weak.

If you want to control a man you have to first earn his trust.

ALWAYS RESPECT HIM IN PUBLIC

Always show respect for your man when you are in public. Do not get into an argument with him. Do not try to contradict him. Do not bring up embarrassing personal things about him. Do not make jokes about him. No matter how innocent a joke might be, it could still be misinterpreted by him, or the people around you. Do not try to demonstrate how independent and strong-willed you are with respect to him. Instead, be sweet at all times when you are with family, friends or strangers. Act like he has you in check. Everyone will admire you more for this. Women will think that he must be doing something right to get you to be so nice. Men will think that he is a very lucky guy. Your man will appreciate the respect you are showing him. He will know that he can trust you when the two of you are out in public. This is very important if you want him to start thinking of you as a marriage partner. No man will trust or allow himself to get too close to a woman who is unpredictable and liable to say or do anything in front of his boss, business partner, close friends or family members. He may keep you around if the sex is good, but he will keep you at arm's length. He will be very conscious of what he confides in you because he knows that it could later blow up in his face. He will be very leery about allowing you around his close friends or important business or political associates. You have little to no chance of establishing control over a man who has learned not to trust you in public.

Remember the Honeymooners? While the relationship between Ralph and Alice may not have been the most ideal, one thing remained consistent, no matter how much Alice yelled at Ralph privately, when they had guests (other than the Nortons) she always showed Ralph the utmost respect. She was the perfect little housewife! This is one of the reasons why Ralph always told her: "Baby you're the greatest!" The scriptwriters of the show knew how important and powerful this quality was for a woman to have.

Avoid voicing your opinions on controversial topics. Do not talk about politics, religion, controversial historical events or other things that could lead to a heated debate. You probably don't know all of your man's views and you are bound to be at odds with him on some issues. This could lead to an unpleasant exchange between the two of you in front of others. The best thing you can do is listen quietly and smile sweetly. While you should avoid voicing your opinion you could instead ask interesting questions. Very often the most intelligent person in the room is the one who asks thought-provoking questions. Ask others, for their opinions. You should especially ask your man what his opinion is. This is a very powerful thing for you to do, because you are letting everyone know that you respect your man's opinion. This will also boost his ego. People love being asked their opinions about things. You will endear yourself to everyone the more you ask them for their opinions. If someone insists on asking what you think about a controversial topic, say something like: "I need to look into it some more before I can form an opinion." You could also say: "The arguments on both sides are very strong, what do you think?"

Have you ever noticed how the wives of politicians act in public with their husbands? What is the dominant recollection you have of them when they are in public with their husbands? You probably recall them quietly smiling sweetly. While some of these women may have been in control behind the scenes, they knew how to conduct themselves in public with their husbands. Such men could not afford to have wives who were unpredictable and a possible public embarrassment. Men of great wealth or political aspirations seek wives whom they can depend on in public settings. While your man may not be rich or running for political office, the same principal applies, always respect him in public and he will treasure you for it.

22

STOP READING MAN-HATING BOOKS AND ARTICLES

Stop reading man hating-books and articles. Material that portrays men as no good, unreliable, shiftless and a host of other things you have already read about countless times before, creates the impression that all men are like this. Enough is enough! The more negativity you fill yourself with the more negative men you are going to have in your life. Ever notice how so many women who are supposed to be so wise about the ways of men having read so much about them, end up in terrible relationships. Since they are so filled with negative thoughts, this is all that they can attract. Likewise, articles that tell women how to get over on men, and play with their feelings and their head, are just another form of negativity. Playing positive games geared towards casting your spell over the man you want is okay, but a lot of articles encourage women to play cruel mind games on men they have no interest in.

I have also found it interesting that a lot of novels and movies which dwell on the worst examples of men, often put a big emphasis on sisterhood or women bonding together. If you would rather be bonding with some women than building a future with the man you want, that is your choice. If you want to attract positive men and have positive relationships, then you must stop reading all of that negative stuff. Flush all of that negative thinking out of your system. Rediscover some of that lost innocence you had. Innocence coupled with a positive outlook is very appealing to men. On countless occasions I have heard men complain that American women don't have any innocence. This is another reason why so many men are traveling around the world seeking wives in other countries. When a man is with a woman who has not been exposed to all of that negativity, he feels like breathing a sigh of relief, because finally he does not have to deal with all of that animosity. Think about it, how inclined would you be to date a guy who has read every woman-hating book and article on the market. Would this be the ideal person for you to be around? It probably would not.

I know you are worrying about being used if you let your guard down, but as I have pointed out before, you don't have to worry about that too much, because you are the one choosing the man you will be with. If you are filled with positive energy, then you will attract and be attracted to positive, hardworking men who appreciate you. If you are filled with negativity, you will attract gamblers, alcoholics, hustlers and abusers. The types of men you are constantly reading about will materialize in your world. It becomes a self-fulfilling prophecy. Remember that you do the choosing. Review Chapter 17 - *Men to Avoid*. Also read Chapter 24 - *Become Relaxed And Centered*. These which will help you generate positive energy within you. Think positive. Forget the negative. Stop fanning the flames of animosity by reading negative man-hating material.

23

CREATE TRANQUILITY

A man wants tranquillity in his home. He wants peace and quiet when he comes home. His home is his escape from all the craziness and hassles of the outside world. Some women are under the misconception that they must constantly nag or do something to provoke an argument in order to keep a man interested. I have heard several women and even some teenage girls express this view. Nothing could be further from the truth, for most men at least. While men love to debate issues whether they involve sports or politics, they don't enjoy constant petty confrontations with their woman.

If there are some men who like constant bickering, why would you want to be around such men? Unless you want your blood pressure constantly going up, don't have anything to do with such men. The average man on the other hand works an average of forty to sixty hours a week on a job he doesn't like and is not being paid what he is worth. Do you really think that he wants to engage in some petty argument when he gets home or is on a date? Given the fact that we are in a two-income economy, the average woman also works all week in a stressful unfulfilling job. Do you really need the additional stress that comes from constant confrontations with your man? Life is too short for all of that nonsense.

Men have weaknesses, and they make all kinds of mistakes. Try to ignore and forgive as many things as you can. If it helps, imagine that you are dating or married to Robert Redford or Denzel Washington, and ask yourself, how much of what they might do wrong, would you find a way to put up with? If you have chosen to pursue or be with a particular man, then he obviously is important enough for you to invest your time and effort in, so why not take the extra effort necessary to reduce confrontations and keep your relationship happy and pleasant.

I have spoken to couples who have been married for thirty years or more and I was amazed to discover that each one stressed the same thing as one of the most important reasons for the longevity of their marriage. They each worked at ways to limit confrontations. One elderly woman told me that when her husband started yelling about something she would just ignore him and go about her business. One elderly man told me that when his wife started fussing he would just leave for a few hours. They each found a way to work around confrontations.

If your man is doing something you don't like, talk to him about it in a sweet and pleasant tone. Offer to make him his favorite dish or give him a full body massage if he could do this one little thing for you. If he persists in doing or not doing something that is bothering you, try to work around it where you correct the problem without him. Think of creative little ways to remind him to do the things that you would like him to do. Obviously all problems can not be resolved so easily, but there are many that could if you put your mind to it.

Every man knows that what a woman does in practice is what she will do in the game. If you are arguing with him all of the time while you are dating, there is a good chance that you will do the same if you got married. Men don't want that kind of aggravation seven days a week. A stressful atmosphere at home is another thing that drives men to seek solitude in the arms of another woman. Constant arguing is what breaks up marriages. Therefore, try to avoid arguments as much as possible.

24

BECOME RELAXED AND CENTERED

The average modern-day woman is extremely stressed out and she brings that stress into her relationship with her man. Since most women are now working the same types of jobs as men, the stress from being in the workforce is increasingly taking its toll on the emotional and physical well being of women. Furthermore, women are cooking less and eating more processed fast foods, which compounds their stress. A man does not need someone who is just as stressed out as he is. A man views a woman as a breath of fresh air from all of the stress that he has to deal with. The more relaxed and spiritually centered you are, the more men will gravitate to you and want to be around you. The more tranquil you are, the calmer you will make him feel.

To become more relaxed you should drastically reduce your intake of soda, coffee, greasy foods, salt, white sugar, very spicy foods, candy, and dairy products. These types of foods keep you hyper, clogged up and unbalanced. Eat more fruits and vegetables of different varieties. Drink fruit and vegetable juices. Buy some books on vegetarian dishes and prepare some delicious vegetarian meals. Try an experiment, for one week, give up all sodas, and instead drink only water, fruit juices and vegetable juices. By the end of the week you will be amazed at how relaxed you will feel. The next week try to also eliminate all meat and dairy products in addition to the sodas. You will be stunned by how much better you will feel. You will not only feel calmer, but you will also have more energy and start to lose weight. You are what you eat.

Drink a lot of distilled water or water from an expensive water purification system. The cheap water purifiers only get out a fraction of the impurities in the water. Look for the ones that remove 95% or more of all of the impurities in your water. Water helps to flush your system out of the toxins that have built up in you.

Consider doing a fast. Fasting is a great way to clean out your system of toxins. You will feel more relaxed and it will add years to your life. There are different types of fasts. For example, there are juice fasts in which you consume various fruit and vegetable juices as well as herbal teas. You should only do a fast under the guidance of organizations that can tailor a specific fasting program for you. Organizations such as the Temple of The Healing Spirit (718-264-9497) and Heal Thyself (718-221-4325), have many years of experience and can guide you through an effective fast. The more you know about your body, the better you will be able to take care of it. The Temple Of The Healing Spirit also has a publication entitled: *The Wounded Womb*, which has a great deal of information that most women are probably not aware of about their body.

Study yoga or meditation or Tai Chi. These ancient techniques have proven their effectiveness over time. They will teach you how to breathe, how to focus and how to relax. Over time you will feel more spiritually attuned and this will reflect in your mannerisms and behavior.

Get a professional full body massage once or twice a month. You will be amazed at how much tension that will be released from a professional massage.

Do some type of exercise at least three to five days a week.

These could include walking, swimming, or bicycling. Join a gym and get an instructor to train you. The key here is that whatever you do, you do it at least three to five days a week.

If you follow these suggestions you will become calmer and more peaceful. Your voice will become softer. You will become less confrontational and better able to avoid arguments. You will radiate warmth and tranquillity. Men desperately need and crave these qualities in a woman. The more of a soothing affect that a woman can have on a man, the more he needs her. The more a man needs a woman, the more control she has over him!

25

MONEY - DON'T TRY TO IMPRESS HIM

Don't try to impress men with how much money you have. Men are more interested in your body than your bank account. In addition, all men know that the more money a woman has, the more lip he is going to have to put up with. Heaven forbid if a woman has more money in the bank or is making more money on her job than her man. Few men are eager to allow themselves to be in such a situation. It is not so much that the average man would be intimidated by how much more money his woman is making, but rather the average modern day woman would feel compelled to constantly give little nasty reminders to her man that she is making more money. This comes out especially when arguments take place. In addition, a woman with too much money is too independent. She can leave the relationship at anytime. This is why men tend to date and marry women who are financially below them or at their same level, but rarely do they seek women who are economically above them.

A man likes to feel that his woman is dependent on his income or at the very least there is interdependence. Money is therefore one more hook he has to keep her by his side. In more ancient times the woman was dependent on the man to hunt for food, and protect her from invading armies. In addition to being a source of dependence, the ability to provide for his woman and his family is a source of great pride for men. Therefore a woman who comes off like she is too self-sufficient, has less appeal for men. There are a lot of successful and even very wealthy women out there who don't have husbands or even boyfriends.

You don't have to give up your high-paying job to become a teacher, or turn over your size-able bank account to charity. Just don't flaunt what you have to a man. You would do better to come off like a working girl just barely able to make ends meet. Don't talk about how well your stock portfolio is doing or how great your real estate investments are going. A woman does not need money to attract or hold the attention of men. Men need money to attract women, especially the ones they want to marry. If there is no way to hide how much money you have because of the type of work you do such as is the case for doctors, lawyers and corporate executives, then act like money is no big deal to you. Money is just a means to an end and that you are really just a down to earth woman. Dress modestly. Avoid wearing a lot of expensive clothing or jewelry when going on casual dates. Remember that a man is more interested in your personality and body than how much money you have.

26

HOW TO ASK FOR SOMETHING

If you follow the guidelines presented here in *The Secrets*, your man will generally be willing to do anything that you ask him. You have become far too valuable and precious for him to risk losing you or hurting your feelings. He knows that it would be a long time, if ever, for him to find a woman as exciting, sensual and able to take care of him as much as you do. His money couldn't even buy a woman as special as you because you have knowledge! You have cast a spell over him, which he doesn't understand, but he doesn't want to give up.

If there is some extra special request which you have, and you want to make it as easy as possible for him to give you a quick yes, then consider the following. First make sure that what you are asking for is well within his ability to comfortably do. Maybe you want to go on an exotic cruise, or you need money or you need him to co-sign for a car. You shouldn't ask for things that are money related if you are unsure if they are well within his means. He will still try to give you what you want to make you happy, but it may take longer for him to do it. Assuming that what you want is well within his means, you must set the atmosphere. Cook him his favorite meal with wine and candlelight. Before, during and after dinner, get him hot and horny by talking dirty, exposing parts of your body, fondling him and using the other suggestions already presented. Once you are sure that he is good and hot, you all of a sudden act like you just remembered something you wanted to ask him which is really important to you. Now you can ask him for what you want. He will agree to almost anything to avoid changing the mood that you are both in. Any hesitation on his part, he knows can lead to a long drawn out discussion, which he doesn't want. Anything short of an immediate "yes" he knows could be a problem, which is the last thing he wants, because all he wants at this point is to get in between your hot thighs!

Once he agrees, fuck his brains out. Think in advance about some of the things you are going to do to him. You should already know some of the things that he likes, so do them. In addition, try a few new things that you think he might enjoy. You could try different positions, different rooms or something kinky like screwing him while he is blindfolded. If you really want to give him an extra special treat, because what he has agreed to is really big or really important to you, consider having a girlfriend or a professional someplace close by waiting for you to signal by cellular phone. When you present the two of you as your token of appreciation he will think that he has died and gone to heaven. Men always fantasize about making love to two women. He will remember the experience for the rest of his life. In addition, he will be eager for you to ask him for something else.

The next day call him at work or leave him a note or a card, thanking him for a wonderful time and for agreeing to whatever you asked for. Now don't have sex with him until he fulfills his commitment or takes a serious step in that direction. If it is a trip to Aruba he has agreed to, wait until he has made the reservations or least begun checking prices. If he has agreed to co-sign on a car loan or to buy you a new car, wait until he has agreed to an appointment with the car dealer. Don't come out and tell him that you won't make love to him until he does such and such.

Instead just come up with nice, plausible excuses why you can't make love to him. One of the easiest excuses is that you are just not feeling well. Another good one is that you are working on a special project from your job. In most cases you won't need to deny him sex for long, because he will probably take the necessary action the very next day or shortly thereafter.

Keep in mind that your man didn't agree to your request just because you asked him after you got him horny. He agreed to it largely because you have been setting the atmosphere for this request long before. You were there for him when he was sick, or just needed to be with you. You don't put a lot of pressure on him nor do a lot of the annoying things that other women do. Sex with you has become an exciting adventure full of delicious surprises. You give him full body massages with warm massage lotion, where as other women wouldn't or didn't take the time to learn how. He enjoys talking to you because you really listen, you have an interest in some of the things that he is interested in, and you ask intriguing questions. In essence you have earned the right to ask him for something you want or need. He knows this and he will be happy to show his appreciation for being the special, enchanting wonderful woman you are.

In the unlikely event that he says no, find out why. Be sure to do this in a nice way. Maybe he really can't afford what you are asking for. Keep in mind that many men try to put up a good financial front for their women. They may spend more money on expensive clothes, colognes, jewelry, and other things that they can't afford. He may be driving a Lexus, but if he is still living with his parents you have to wonder. That is why you must make sure that what you want is well within his means. If you are married, you should have a pretty good idea of his financial picture. If money is not the issue, then principle or extreme inconvenience may be the problem. Hopefully you did not ask him to rob a bank or kill a former lover. Maybe he has already agreed to marry you, but he is a Buddhist and you want to get married in a Christian Church. If the issue is principle, then listen objectively to his reasoning and politely talk about it in a truly loving and understanding way. He will appreciate this. If the issue is extreme inconvenience, listen closely to what he is saying. Maybe he really can't take the time off from work to go somewhere. If in the final analysis you see that he is sincere and there is some logic or credibility in his reasoning, just tell him in a sweet tone that you understand. Let the tone of your voice and expression, softly convey your disappointment. Kiss him sweetly, and hug him, but don't make love to him on the same night. Let him know that your mood has changed, but still cuddle up to him and be affectionate. If the two of you have been in a long discussion over why he can't grant your request, his mood has probably changed too. By treating him in this way, you will make him feel guilty. Don't be surprised if he calls you the next day and tells you that he will do it. If he really can't do that particular thing he will work very hard at trying to do other things to make it up to you.

If a guy comes out and just tells you no, and refuses to even discuss it with you, dump him! If he does not appreciate you enough and respect you enough to at least give you an explanation, you don't need him. He is a moron! He has a high opinion of himself and a low opinion of you. You should feel lucky that you found out how he really is before you wasted more time on him.

Keep in mind that it is extremely unlikely that your man will say no to a reasonable request if you have been setting the atmosphere all along by following the guidelines that have been presented here. He will be happy to do something for you that you really want. You are his very special lady!

THE GREATEST SECRET OF ALL

Deep down men love women!!! It is more than just sex, it is a deep appreciation for what women are - women! Men love to listen to the sound of women's voices. They love how women smell and feel. They love the very essence of womanhood.

A woman is more than just a man with different body parts. A woman is a principle, a special energy that compliments the male energy. A man can not be complete without a woman. Women are the mothers of the human race. The burden they take on for nine months no man would want to bear. The responsibilities they take on as mothers and wives are awesome. While the average man will not talk about this, he appreciates and has a deep, sincere respect for women.

Women offer another perspective and approach to understanding and coping with the world, which complements men. The two principles combined are far more powerful than they are alone. This is why married men tend to live longer healthier lives than single men do. This is why children who grow up in families in which both parents are present, tend to be more emotionally and psychologically balanced and spiritually centered. Intuitively men understand this, which is why they truly love women deep down. When a man sees a woman his innate impulse is to love, respect and protect. While women have a strong innate desire to be nurturing, a man has a desire to protect and provide for women. Wars have been fought over women. Men have killed and have sacrificed themselves for women.

A woman who understands this, understands the power she has over men. Such a woman can walk into a room and have men stumbling over themselves trying to appease her. Such a woman seems to send out a psychic signal that is non-threatening, but nonetheless commands respect and admiration by virtue of the fact that she is a woman. Few men would dare to sit while such a woman was standing. I have found that women who are versed in traditional cultural values have a far better understanding of their power over men and how to direct their power in positive ways.

Their power stems from the fact that they understand the interdependence of men and women. They respect, need and love men. They know that a woman is not whole without a man. They don't buy into the modern "I'm independent; I don't need a man" madness. They know that men and women were put here to be together in harmony. When they are not together, chaos brews, madness sinks in and society starts to crumble. The male and female relationship is the basis for the family, which is the basis for the community and society. The more discord there is between men and women, the more chaos exists in society. America has the highest divorce rate in the world, and look at all of the massive problems that exist on all levels of American society.

The few women who understand all of this also understand that not only do women and men compliment each other, but they also have different roles. The man is suppose to love, respect, protect and provide for women, just as women are suppose to be nurturing, comforting and bringing forth life. She does not see herself as in competition with men, because men are suppose to tend to her need for security and other things. Men have their role and women have theirs. That's it! Even in the context of our modern industrial society where men can't go out and hunt for food for their family, but have to work for someone else, these women recognize all of this, but still maintain the same basic respect for men and expect the same in return. You may be asking yourself how is all of this possible, because the men you have met did not show you that kind of respect and most wouldn't even give a woman a seat on a bus. The secret is simple. You must change your attitude. If you walk around thinking that men are dumb and easily taken advantage of, it shows. If your goal is to just get what you can out of a man and then toss him to the side - it shows. If you are carrying a lot of negative garbage from past relationships into your new relationship - it shows! A woman who is filled with negative thoughts and is always plotting and planning to take advantage of the men they encounter, give themselves away in their facial features, mannerisms and general aura. Her facial features are tense instead of calm and relaxed. Her eyes are probing and analytical like a panther sizing up its prey before pouncing! You must drop all of that negativity and replace it with love and respect. If you do this you will generate positive energy. A consistent theme in the self-help books is that if a person harbors a lot of negativity within themself, he or she will attract negative people and negative situations. On the other hand, those who are positive, generate positive energy, and attract positive people and positive situations. If you have a truly loving and giving personality, men will see these qualities and gravitate to you.

You don't have to worry too much about some men taking advantage of you because women do the choosing when it comes to relationships. Men can only pick from among those women who consider them to be a candidate. You will only get involved with or stay involved with a jerk if you choose to. Women who are filled with animosity gravitate to such men and attract such men. If you are truly positive you won't be attracted to weak manipulative men. Instead you will inspire the best in men and draw the best to you. Men love women, but it is up to each individual woman to draw the best out of men in general and their man in particular.

SUMMARY

The average woman can exercise tremendous power over the average man. A woman can inflame the passions of a man so much that he will make any sacrifice for her, including laying down his own life. A man can create or destroy empires with the right woman who knows how to cast the right spells over his heart, mind, soul and of course his dick! A man who is properly motivated would go to any lengths to please such a woman and make sure that all of her needs and desires are taken care of. Unfortunately, most women don't realize how much power they have or how to effectively exercise it. This is unfortunate because most men are willing to step up to the plate and be a warrior and provider for the right woman. The average woman can have almost any man she wants and have him eating out of her hands while loving every minute of it. Therefore, reread this book several times until you really absorb the information. Follow the guidelines presented along with a little common sense and see what happens! You now have *The Secrets* - use them!

ABOUT THE AUTHOR

Mr. Cost writes and lectures on various social issues. He has been featured in The New York Times, The Village Voice, The Amsterdam News and other publications. He has also been interviewed on the national television talk show: Tony Brown's Journal, as well as numerous cable and radio talk shows.